Capitol Hill Library

JAN 14 2020

THE
Beer
PANTRY

THE *Beer* PANTRY

COOKING AT THE INTERSECTION *of* CRAFT BEER AND GREAT FOOD

Adam Dulye *with* Michael Harlan Turkell

DOVETAIL

DOVETAIL

Text copyright © 2018 by Adam Dulye and Michael Harlan Turkell
Photographs copyright © 2018 by Scott Gordon Bleicher
Design and illustrations by Carolyn Håkansson
Food styling by Olivia Mack Anderson

Published by Dovetail Press in Brooklyn, New York, a division of Assembly Brands LLC.

For details or ordering information, contact the publisher at the address below or email info@dovetail.press.

Dovetail Press
42 West Street #403
Brooklyn, NY 11222
www.dovetail.press

Library of Congress Cataloging-in-Publication data is on file with the publisher.
ISBN: 978-0-99873-998-4
First printing, March 2018
Printed in China
10 9 8 7 6 5 4 3 2 1

CONTENTS

FOREWORD

By Joshua M. Bernstein

Man can't live on beer alone. Trust me. I've tried.

Over the last 15 years, beer has been my writing beat, taking me from Washington's Yakima Valley to sip fresh-hopped pale ales, to Vermont for fruity and hazy IPAs, and Prague, where the unfiltered pilsners are especially lovely.

Hoisting half liters of superfresh lager is heavenly, but it's only half the equation. Every excellent beer deserves a great culinary mate to keep the days going round and round, round after round. Perhaps it's grilled clams with a couple of cans of Firestone Walker Brewing Company's Pivo Pils, or maybe a medium-rare burger with that timeless, classic Sierra Nevada Brewing Co.'s Pale Ale. What about carrot cake with a wondrous IPA, like, say, Russian River Brewing Company's Blind Pig? Heck, I'll take any suggestion from chef Adam Dulye. He's a beer-pairing wizard of the highest order.

I first tasted Adam's matching mastery at SAVOR, the Brewers Association's annual culinary-minded beer festival. Yazoo's smoky, bourbon barrel–aged Fortuitous porter found harmony with a roasted beet and chèvre tartlet finished with a sherry gastrique, while Avery's vinous Muscat D'Amour partnered with a crème puff crammed with huckleberry and Meyer lemon. SAVOR crushed the misconception that beer is bubbly stuff served by the pitcher with a basket of chicken wings.

Adam's feats of culinary derring-do left me awed, and stuffed, a regular occurrence over the last decade. We fermented a friendship, the chef and the writer, and he became my beer–food sage. Adam supplied me with spot-on pairing advice for my second book, *Complete Beer Course*. When I wrote about sour beers for *Bon Appétit*, Adam offered up sterling couplings like gueuze with country-style pâté. Session IPAs with lime-squeezed fish tacos? That was Adam's suggestion in my third book, *Complete IPA*.

And now it's time for Adam's first book.

Countless beer-focused cookbooks counsel cooks to add beer to everything, glugging stouts into chili, adding Scotch ales to stews, steaming mussels in a lake's worth of witbier.

Trouble is, a beer's unique profile often disappears in the flavorful muddle and all that precious alcohol evaporates into the ether.

The Beer Pantry takes a different tack. Adam doesn't advocate dumping lagers into everything willy-nilly. Instead, he's created recipes that preach technique and quality ingredients over cramming a beer can inside a chicken and calling it a day. Beer is only employed when it plays a key role, such as the brown ale–glazed figs that are gangbusters with bone-in pork chops (see page 88). Care for Chardonnays more than IPAs? No matter. Despite the book's title, dishes like sautéed chanterelles with roasted fennel (see page 51) can stand by their lonesome, no liquid accompaniment required.

Match those mushrooms with Dogfish Head's malty 60-Minute IPA, though, and you'll amplify the fungi's savory earthiness, unlocking new depths of flavor. Food and beer are two key pieces of a culinary puzzle, incomplete without each other. A great meal deserves an equally great beer. Adam intimately understands this synergy. It's time to stock *The Beer Pantry* in your kitchen, preferably next to a couple of great six-packs.

After all, you're not really living if you're living on food alone.

—Joshua M. Bernstein is the author of Brewed Awakening, Complete Beer Course, Complete IPA, *and* Homebrew World.

INTRODUCTION

I remember fishing in the Pacific Northwest during a steelhead run. It was summer, a day off with a sous chef who was an avid fisherman. It was 95 degrees out; my legs were ice cold in the river's current, and I grabbed a crisp bottle of kölsch. We'd brought with us a smattering of food, since catching fish is never a guarantee, but once we hooked one, our excitement was real. We chopped fillets into a simple tartare and ate it off chilled cucumber slices. The subsequent sip of beer acted as the perfect peppery seasoning. For me, this is when beer and food became one.

When I roast a duck breast and its sweet caramel scent perfumes the air, I always have a toasty brown ale in hand, much the same way I make sure there's a citrusy saison on the picnic table whenever I'm lucky enough to have a bowl of buttery Dungeness crab. I always follow shucked oysters, glistening in their briny liquor, with a swig of a dry stout. I hope this book will inspire you to find your own "compulsory" pairings, drawing new parallels between beer and food. They speak similar languages and only benefit from one another's presence at the table.

This is a book about cooking *for* beer, not necessarily *with* beer. There are a few recipes, like Chicken Liver and Quadrupel Ale Mousse (see page 158), and a riff on the Burgundian class Coq au Vin (made with saison, see page 147) that are made better by the inclusion of beer, while other recipes include ingredients used in the actual brewing process, like Radishes Dipped in Hop Butter (see page 21), or Malted Oat Pecan Cookies (see page 125). But I want to stress that "beer food" doesn't have to contain beer in order to go with it.

Chefs have long used complementary and contrasting flavors as a way of building dishes. This book will stock your pantry with simple condiments and provide recipes that not only celebrate great food and beer, but also help you work toward understanding the connections between food and beer flavor profiles. Next time you're sipping a sour beer, you'll know to go for gorgonzola, or when you're having something spicy, balance it out with an IPA. Being able to dial in these couplings will result in "pairings" in the truest sense of the word, being able to recognize that two things go together, and should be inextricably attached. I'll drink, and eat, to that!

My association with beer and food started during my time in Vail, Colorado, a couple of decades ago. I was a young cook, working endless hours prepping for lengthy wine pairing dinners at luxury resorts. Please don't mistake me for a beer-centrist. I do enjoy wine, and cocktails, but I've listened to one too many long-winded commentaries about how some big-ticket wine has notes of this and that, and how its minerality boosted the presence of some exclusive ingredient in the dish. I believed the point of all this jargon was purely to sell expensive wine; these pairings felt more like marketing stories than synergy. That said, the Rockies were fertile ground for many breweries, and the chefs I was working with were no longer relegating beer to a shift drink. They were exploring a growing number of styles and flavors—a far cry from the pale-yellow lagers our parents grew up on. These new craft brewers were a different breed and, like my generation of chefs, they, too, were engaged in local, seasonal, and sustainable practices. They were community-focused and collaborative, and they challenged their competitors as friends rather than foes, strengthening the industry and keeping it congenial, over a beer.

At that point in my culinary career, I hadn't come across anyone in the industry who was pairing beers with a fine dining menu. Beer was an *après ski* beverage, a pre-dinner drink, or something you had when you were outside grilling. The door was blown wide open when in the late 1990s brewers began playing with more food-friendly styles: brown ales, wheat beers, and balanced hoppy ones. When I tasted these beers, I knew they weren't just for drinking; they had notes of caramel and toffee, herbs, salt, pepper. It was a lexicon I inherently knew from cooking, and could relate back to my pantry. Beer was finding its way into the culinary world through a shared flavor language.

Then this whole "cooking with beer" became a thing. Suddenly it was cool to add any beer to any dish and be all, "Look at me, I'm cooking with beer." When cooking, ask yourself one question: does an ingredient make the dish taste better? If so, good. If not, don't do it. If you go back and ask that question about most well-known recipes for cooking with beer, the answer will most likely be no.

Because of this, beer was pigeonholed into a realm of gimmicky food. Eleven-Beer Chili? Come on! You can't possibly taste eleven beers in a single stewed pot of ground meat. You're just wasting beer! Beer Cheese Soup is composed of a roux and cheese, sometimes with potato as a thickener, all of which will mask any beer's flavor. And then there's Beer-Can Chicken where the can itself is more of a prop than anything. A chicken doesn't need to be upright to stay juicy on a grill; you're better off drinking that beer.

But pair a brown ale with a duck breast that's been perfectly seared and drizzled with a sharp gastrique? Or steam mussels with a smooth Belgian witbier, its slight honey-like flavor augmenting the natural sweetness of seafood . . . now you're talking. Cooking is steeped in technique, and the ultimate goal is to develop flavor without compromising the integrity of the ingredients.

The United States is internationally celebrated as fertile ground of the modern craft beer movement and credited with creating entirely new styles of beer. According to the Brewers Association, there are now more than 100 distinct U.S. beer styles, from India Pale Ales to barrel-aged sours.

Obviously, there are still plenty of American lagers made by megaproducers. These are essentially identical products, simply made for expediency and profit, but today, the U.S. has more than 5,000 breweries, of which 99 percent are small and independent. The majority of Americans live within 10 miles of a brewery. Each of the 50 states has a brewer's guild, of which many organize their own annual beer week to celebrate local breweries. More than 2,000 future breweries are planned or under construction at the time of writing. The thirst for American craft beer continues to grow internationally and has begun to attract and influence the global beer market with its unique styles and flavors.

Our modern food culture has progressed along a similar trajectory. No longer satisfied with mass-market goods, there's been a big shift toward a future full of local, organic, and sustainable food businesses. Farmers' markets have become more popular than ever, CSA shares are finding their way into more households, and both gourmet food markets and grocery chains are taking greater care in what they put on their shelves. With that, craft beer shelves are now lined with more regional brews than ever before.

But when it comes to choosing what to drink with a meal, most cooks and diners still reach for wine out of reflex. Let's exercise our drinking muscles and bring beer to the table.

Just as brewing techniques are set for each style (e.g., kölsch should taste like kölsch whether it's made in Cologne or in California), cooking has fundamental ways of building flavors. If you need to deglaze a pan, there is a proper way to do that. Need acid to sharpen a dish? There is a technique for that as well.

"Beer is a food." That's what Charlie Papazian, the founder of the Brewers Association and Great American Beer Festival, said during a 1994 Chef to Chef conference in Las Vegas. His presentation was entitled, "About What's Going On In America With Beer," and the three biggest takeaways were:

1   Beer can essentially replace liquid in many recipes.

2   Beer enhances the flavor of food without taking center stage.

3   Beer's wide range of styles can complement varying degrees of food's flavors and strengths.

I've said my piece about the first one, but I entirely agree with the other two. Beer is fuel for food, a companion made to pair and flatter flavors, not detract from them. Certain beer and food combinations work just as innately as benchmark wine pairings, such as Champagne and caviar or Zinfandel and short ribs.

In my time as a chef, it's been my mission to bring my beer and food pairing philosophies to the forefront, educating drinkers and diners alike, that matching characteristics like carbonization with salinity and pairing high ABV (alcohol by volume) with fat can prosper. When I cooked in restaurants, or even at beer and food events with the

Brewers Association, I loved seeing people arrive at the conclusion that a yeasty beer goes well with seafood or that big fruity ones work perfectly with proteins.

As beer is becoming more ingredient-driven, more fine dining restaurants such as Gramercy Tavern in New York, The Red Hen in Washington, D.C., Higgins in Portland, Spur in Seattle, and even Eleven Madison Park, named best restaurant in the world, are paying attention. Each of these have highly curated, multipaged beer lists featuring small production, one-off experimental beers, and even cellars of more classic reserved bottles. The world of haute cuisine has not only noticed craft beer, it's embraced it.

And now, many of the country's best chefs are collaborating with breweries to make signature beers for their restaurants. The French Laundry's Thomas Keller worked with Brooklyn Brewery's Garret Oliver to make a "Blue Apron" Dubbel; chef Masaharu Morimoto collaborated with Oregon's Rogue to make a soba-based ale; in Washington, D.C., José Andrés offers a Spanish-inspired saison created for him by Deschutes from Portland, Oregon, and chef Jamie Bissonnette of Toro and Coppa in New York City and Boston, teamed up with New Hampshire's Smuttynose Brewing Company to make a limited run of "Pure Biss," a Belgian-style witbier, that was flavored with kaffir lime leaves, spruce, and grapefruit.

The beer and culinary worlds are no longer autonomous. For example, Short's Brewing Company made a "Bloody Beer" that was fermented with Roma tomatoes, spiced with dill, horseradish, peppercorns, and celery. I've picked green peppercorns while brewing a beer with Dogfish Head's Sam Calagione; the "Beard de Garde," a tribute to James Beard. Right Brain Brewing Company in Traverse City, Michigan, has ended the debate that nothing can pair with asparagus by making their Spear Beer Asparagus Ale.

Rather than deciding to make culinary-minded beers, I aspire to make food that's beer-minded. When it comes to pairing craft beer and food, the rules are much less rigid than with wine. The presence of carbonization and bittering agents enables beer to cleanse the palate in a way that wine with its acidity and tannins can't. Thanks to the wide range of ingredients available to craft brewers, they're able to dial in flavors in a way that winemakers can't.

I've had the privilege of learning from so many pioneering beer makers that it would be a shame not to introduce them to you—throughout the book you'll learn about them in the Brewer Spotlight sections. Their beers have helped me become a better cook, and with their guidance, I've been able to break down beer styles into six flavor profiles for efficiency's sake, which I call the "Six-Pack": Crisp & Clean, Hoppy & Bitter, Malty & Sweet, Rich & Roasty, Fruity & Spicy, and lastly, Sour, Tart, & Funky. The subsequent chapters are divided into these flavor profiles, which food conveniently falls into as well. I've carefully and personally selected a few beers per recipe that represent the most superlative and diverse craft beer in the country; while you might not be able to find these beers in your market, you can use them as points of reference to find similar styles locally available to you. Consider them guidelines, not rules. But before we even get there, we have to be able to identify flavors in beer and food.

TASTE BUDS
Associating Flavor Through Sensorial Observation

To start, let's dissect where flavor comes from in beer. The combination of carbonation, hops, malt, water, and yeast determines how a beer will taste. Brewers' personal touches throughout the brewing process can also change the character of the resulting beer: color, aroma, carbonation, and body.

When pairing beer with food, I like to consider a beer's flavor profile rather than being guided by its style. It's much easier to talk about beer with words like crisp, clean, bitter, fruity, tart, and sour than with beer-specific terminology like IPA, amber, stout, or pilsner.

COLOR

Most beer is made with four ingredients: hops, malted grain, yeast, and water. The extent to which malt grains are roasted will determine the darkness of the beer. The length of time a beer is boiled during the fermentation process will also affect the depth of color the beer takes on. A longer extraction period of the malts tends to result in a deeper hue.

We tend to associate light colors with lighter beers, caramel colors with sweet flavors, and dark brews with heaviness, but color can play tricks on the mind and palate. While these visual assumptions can sometimes be true, it is also possible to have a dark-colored beer that tastes and feels light, a light-colored beer that boasts rich and complex flavors, or a caramel-colored beer that tastes dry and bitter. In everything but sours, the gradation goes from pale yellow, through amber and brown, to jet black.

There is a Standard Reference Method, or SRM, for beer that assigns a number to the shades, starting at Berliner weisse and witbeirs and going up to imperial stouts. This color scale rates beer's color intensity, so filtration can also factor into this equation. Hazy or cloudy beers are thought to have more saturated tones, but can still be light.

In regard to sours, their colors can come from the addition of fruit, ranging from light watermelon pink, to sour cherry red, and end in a deep jammy purple.

AROMA

A beer's aroma is created through the marriage of hops and malts. Hops are flowers from the *Humulus lupulus* plant, and when steeped in beer, impart a flavorful effect. Certain hops have specific roles too: there are aroma-first varieties, like Cascade (citrus and spicy) and Citra (which is more tropical), then bittering ones like Nugget (which is still earthy and herbal). Fresh hop beers use more aroma hops then bittering ones. Hops with higher alpha acids are more bitter, Chinook being one of the highest, Saaz the lowest. Malts smell sweet, triggering your nerves to make you salivate. Yeast strains (of which there are thousands) can also add to the bouquet. Evaluating the aroma of a beer is done a little differently from wine. First, you don't want to swirl or agitate your beer before you smell it because you're letting flavor escape. Beer is a much more volatile liquid than wine, and because of carbonation, the vapors disperse and dissipate more quickly, which means that you don't have to stick your nose right in the glass. Hold the glass about a few inches from your face. The aromas of beer are much harder to detect when the beer is very cold, so ideally test and taste your beer around 50°F.

CARBONATION

Carbon dioxide (CO_2) is a byproduct of fermentation, produced when yeast converts sugar to alcohol, as seen in those tiny bubbles going up the side of your glass. They're active in a saison, farmhouse, or pilsner, while a lot of sours also have naturally occurring effervescence. Lightly carbonated beers like ambers, stouts, and porters will sit heavier and longer on your palate, while more intensely carbonated beers will invigorate and refresh it. Bubbles lift the aroma of a beer into the nostrils. Every bubble is full of aroma, waiting to hit the palate and pop. Due to this fact, you won't need to slosh beer around in your mouth to make its flavor travel. Note: The colder the beer, the sharper and more intense the feeling of carbonization, so consider temperature here too. Carbonization resets a palate in pairing, cutting through fattiness in food, or helps subdue the heat of something spicy.

PALETTE/BODY

Proteins and residual sugars from the malts, extracted during the brewing process and modified during fermentation, are what determine a beer's body or texture—how it feels in your mouth and on your tongue. It's easiest to think about the body of a beer compared with different types of milk: skim milk (light body), whole milk (medium body), and whipping cream (heavy body). One great indicator of texture is the length of time the head, or foam, of a beer stays thick after it's been poured. The longer it's there, the smoother the body will be. The head on a pilsner tends to be light and airy and will disappear much faster than that of a stout.

Beer has a start and finish, just like wine does. On first sip, you'll taste the malt build (the specific combination of grains used to make a beer), then the hops will come into focus, and after that, carbonization comes into play. IPAs are balanced and bitter, stouts are roasty and bitter and finish smooth and creamy. These textures appear in food too of course, and sometimes you'll need to pair a heavy dish with a light beer.

ROB TOD

ALLAGASH BREWERY

Allagash has been making beer in Maine since 1995. With over 100 employees, anyone, regardless of department, can talk with the brewmaster and make a 10-gallon batch. Lots of full-scale innovative releases have been born out of this program, and that's at the core of what founder Rob Tod is all about. A lot of their beers fall into the Crisp & Clean bucket; they're very drinkable, but also give the brewer lots of room for creating balance and complexity. The brewer can easily incorporate subtle characteristics into these beers because of their simple backdrop. The challenge for Tod was keeping an open mind; when first dipping his toes into barrel aging, he assumed only dark beers would work with bourbon barrels. Maybe that's because the few barrel-aged beers that were available back then were dark? Maybe it was just an assumption that it would take big roasted flavors to stand up to the oak and bourbon notes? One day they ran out of bottles during a tripel bottling run, so they filled up a couple bourbon barrels with tripel that would have otherwise been dumped. They were blown away by the result! Huge coconut, vanilla, bourbon, and dill notes worked perfectly with the light-colored tripel, and since then, they've had an open mind as to what might work. The same goes for beer with food. Try tripel with a beef stew instead of the typical stout or porter. It provides so many contrasting and complementary flavors, creating a much richer food pairing experience.

ON DRAFT

ALLAGASH WHITE

With such composed carbonation, this beer is refreshing and delicate. It really can be drunk anywhere or anytime. It goes well with fresh herbs (tarragon, basil), clams, mussels, and steamed lobster because it's from Maine!

CHAPTER 01

CRISP & CLEAN

This set of beers refreshes your palate: you don't need to think about them, just drink them and be ecstatically happy. If you ever are perplexed about what to drink next, this is a good choice to consider.

These beers are delicate, slightly dry, and don't overpower, letting the subtler notes speak. There's a nice balance of hop and malt, flavors of green apple and pear. These brews, like pilsners, blonde ales, and kölsch, can go with foods made in a variety of different cooking methods without overwhelming the dish. Amber lagers, German styles like helles, märzen, and maibock, have a little more complexity, toastier malts, and are often nuanced with spring and fall flavors, pairing well with garden vegetables, citrus salads, and fresh seafood.

These beers work well with foods that benefit from a crisp pop of carbonation that scrubs the palate; anything with a bright note, light salt, or vegetable flavor can work well here. Common citrus notes also work well and naturally complement these beers' flavor profiles. Salinity and carbonation respond well to the herbal notes of hops, which helps enhance the food. At the end, the combination of these elements wakes you up, giving you energy to eat and drink more. Lighter fats like olive oil work really well with carbonation, and have a scrubbing feeling: when fat settles on your tongue, carbonation finds its way underneath and lifts it off. In bigger beers (such as stouts and porters), carbonation comes in like a Zamboni and works front to back, whereas these beers work in pockets so they don't overwhelm the palate all at once.

SOME CRISP & CLEAN
BEER STYLES

Amber Lager

Blonde Ale

Helles

Kölsch

Maibock

Märzen

Pilsner

21

RADISHES DIPPED IN HOP BUTTER

22

MARINATED CUCUMBER SALAD

25

SNAPPER CEVICHE WITH CORN AND FENNEL

26

FRIED ZUCCHINI WITH LEMON AND PIQUILLO PEPPER AIOLI

28

EGGPLANT PARMESAN ARANCINI WITH SLOW-COOKED TOMATO SAUCE

30

GRILLED CORN, FENNEL, AND ARUGULA SALAD WITH PARMESAN VINAIGRETTE

32

DUNGENESS CRAB WITH AVOCADO AND GRAPEFRUIT

34

GRILLED CLAMS WITH SPICY CORN AND GARLIC AIOLI

36

GRILLED SALMON WITH HEIRLOOM TOMATOES, FRIED MUSHROOMS, AND ROUILLE

38

OLIVE OIL–POACHED HALIBUT WITH FENNEL, GREEN OLIVES, AND LEMON

CRISP & CLEAN
FOOD FRIENDS

Apple, avocado, clams, coriander, cucumber, fennel, fried foods, ginger, green beans, green onion, leek, lemon, lime, mozzarella, potato, radish, sesame, shallot, tomato, turnip, white fish

RADISHES DIPPED IN HOP BUTTER

Several years ago, I harvested fresh hops at a farm with my friends from Steamworks Brewing in Paonia, Colorado. After picking hop flowers off the bines all day, we went through the vegetable fields and picked ingredients to be cooked over an open fire for dinner. On a whim, we added some fresh hops to melted butter and dipped freshly picked radishes in the mixture, licking the hop flavor right off our fingers after every one. This dish, with a cold kölsch (and a pushy goat, but that's another story) brings me right back to Paonia.

2 bunches small radishes, preferably French Breakfast

½ pound (2 sticks) unsalted butter

2 to 3 wholecone hops or 2 teaspoons hop pellets

Pinch of freshly grated lemon zest

Kosher salt

Freshly ground black pepper

Makes 4 to 6 servings

Trim the bottom of each radish, making sure to leave any healthy tops intact, and set aside.

In a saucepan, melt the butter over low heat, then add the hops. Make sure to keep the butter on low enough heat to ensure that it doesn't break. Remove the pan from the heat and let cool to room temperature. Strain the hops out and discard them.

Transfer the butter to the bowl of a stand mixer fitted with the paddle attachment and whip the butter until it's light and fluffy. Fold in the lemon zest and season to taste with salt and pepper.

Dip each radish in the butter; coat about half of the radish if your radishes are mellow, or coat the whole radish if they have a stronger flavor. Smooth the butter with the back of a spoon to evenly coat the radish, and transfer to a parchment-lined platter. Refrigerate until the butter has formed a glossy coating around the radishes. Serve the radishes on a platter with extra hop butter on the side.

PAIRING STRATEGY

Think of radishes as an extra kick of aromatic hops. If the bite of the radishes is too strong, it will completely dominate the flavor of the beer. If you have a very spicy radish, choose a very hoppy beer. Take a bite of radish first, then sip the beer to notice how these straightforward flavors improve each other's minimalism.

RECOMMENDED BEERS

Prima Pils, Victory Brewing Company
Joe's Pils, Avery Brewing Co.
El Sully, 21st Amendment Brewery

MARINATED CUCUMBER SALAD

I'm happy to eat these crunchy, quick-pickled cucumbers on their own as a snack or small salad, but they're also a good shared side for any meal that needs a palate refresher, like fried chicken, pulled pork, or pan-seared salmon. The marinade is a little bit tart, a little bit sweet, and the onions give it a little bite, making it a perfect reset button.

Makes 4 servings

In a small saucepan, combine the vinegars, 1 teaspoon salt, and sugar. Bring to a boil, then turn off the heat. Let cool to room temperature.

In a bowl, combine the cucumbers, onion, celery seeds, and dill. Pour the cooled vinegar over the cucumber mixture and toss to coat. Refrigerate until ready to serve, at least 4 hours and up to 24 hours. Serve in a small bowl.

½ cup white wine vinegar or champagne vinegar

2 tablespoons rice wine vinegar

Kosher salt

1 teaspoon granulated sugar

2 pounds mini seedless Persian cucumbers, cut into ¼-inch-thick rounds

1 small red onion, thinly sliced

¼ teaspoon celery seeds

¼ cup dill, chopped

PAIRING STRATEGY

The texture and crisp snap of pickled cucumbers act as a palate cleanser in the same way Crisp & Clean beers do. And they taste great together, too.

RECOMMENDED BEERS

Pony Pilsner, Half Acre Beer Company
Seacoast Pilsner, Coronado Brewing Company
Namaste White, Dogfish Head Craft Brewery

SNAPPER CEVICHE WITH CORN AND FENNEL

This dish takes me back to a trip to Lisbon, Portugal, where the ceviche offerings are determined by what comes in on the fishing boats that day. I remember thinking how clean the fish tasted, so extremely fresh. You don't want to mess too much with such perfection, but I've found that corn and fennel have similar and complementary flavors, ones that refresh your palate. All you need is a good squeeze of lime and a little kick of jalapeño to bring it all together.

Makes 4 servings

In a bowl, whisk together the lime juice, 1 tablespoon of the olive oil, jalapeño, garlic, 1/2 teaspoon salt, and pepper. Add the snapper and toss until evenly coated. Cover and refrigerate for at least 8 hours or up to overnight.

Right before you're ready to serve the ceviche, prepare the other vegetables. In a medium skillet, warm the remaining olive oil over medium heat. Add the corn and cook, stirring frequently until tender, 2 to 3 minutes. Add the onion, fennel, and garlic scapes and remove from the heat. Let the mixture cool to room temperature.

Place the corn mixture on the bottom of a plate and scatter the snapper over the top. Garnish with the parsley and fennel fronds, spoon the leftover snapper marinade over the top, and serve immediately.

2 tablespoons fresh lime juice

2 tablespoons olive oil

1 tablespoon jalapeño, seeded and finely chopped

1 garlic clove, finely chopped

Kosher salt

1/8 teaspoon freshly ground black pepper

1/2 pound skinless snapper fillet, cut into 1/2-inch dices or strips

2 ears of corn, kernels removed from the cob

1/2 red onion, thinly sliced

1 medium bulb fennel, cored and thinly sliced, fronds reserved for garnish

1/4 cup thinly sliced garlic scapes

1 tablespoon chopped parsley

PAIRING STRATEGY

This ceviche highlights what the carbonation of beer can do with raw proteins, playing off not only flavors, but textures too. The citrus acidity excites the palate, matching the intensity of the beer and leaving you wanting another bite to figure out what's happening.

RECOMMENDED BEERS

Stammtisch, Urban Chestnut Brewing Company
Mexican Logger, Ska Brewing Company
Cougar Bait, Country Boy Brewing

FRIED ZUCCHINI WITH LEMON AND PIQUILLO PEPPER AIOLI

Every cook goes through a phase of frying anything and everything (some never stop). It's fried zucchini that has really stuck with me. The crispy rounds can add texture (and even some height when piled up) to a dish like grilled whole fish, and make an addictive snack served on their own. I make a dipping sauce to go with the zucchini—it has some heat and sweetness, both of which it gets from piquillo peppers.

Makes 4 to 6 servings

Gently season the zucchini with salt and the lemon juice to extract their moisture, which will help in the breading process. Let the zucchini rest for 15 minutes, then pat dry with a paper towel.

Beat the eggs in a shallow bowl and season with salt and pepper.

Place the flour in another shallow bowl and season with salt and pepper. Place the breadcrumbs in a third bowl. Coat a zucchini slice in flour, then dredge it in the egg mixture, letting the excess run off, then coat in breadcrumbs. Transfer to a platter and repeat with the remaining zucchini.

Heat the canola oil in a medium skillet or medium saucepan until an inserted instant-read thermometer reads 350°F. Working with a few slices at a time, carefully place the zucchini in oil and fry until golden brown, about 2 to 3 minutes. Transfer to a paper towel–lined baking sheet and repeat with the remaining zucchini.

Just before serving, sprinkle the fried zucchini with the lemon zest. Serve immediately with the lemon wedges and the aioli on the side for dipping.

2 pounds medium zucchini, ends trimmed, and cut into ¼-inch-thick rounds

Kosher salt

Finely grated zest and juice of 2 lemons

3 large eggs

Freshly ground black pepper

1 cup all-purpose flour

3 cups fresh breadcrumbs

2 cups canola or grapeseed oil, for frying

Lemon wedges, for serving

Lemon and Piquillo Pepper Aioli, for serving (recipe follows)

PAIRING STRATEGY

The carbonation of Crisp & Clean beers is always great with fried foods, but it's their subtlety of flavor that really lets the taste of the zucchini stand out.

RECOMMENDED BEERS

Brau Pils, DC Brau Brewing Company
Seafarer Kölsch, Three Weavers Brewing Company
Fat Tire Amber Ale, New Belgian Brewing Company

LEMON AND
PIQUILLO PEPPER AIOLI

Makes 1 cup

In the bowl of a food processor, combine the egg yolks, garlic, lemon juice, and piquillo peppers. Purée until smooth, scraping down the bowl as needed. With the machine running, slowly add the canola oil, followed by the olive oil; the mixture should emulsify into a smooth aioli. If the aioli is too thick, add 1 tablespoon of water and blend until the sauce is thinned. Season to taste with salt and refrigerate until ready to use. The aioli will keep in an airtight container, refrigerated, for up to three days.

2 egg yolks

1 garlic clove, thinly sliced

Juice of 1 lemon

¼ cup piquillo peppers

½ cup canola oil

2 tablespoons olive oil

Kosher salt

EGGPLANT PARMESAN ARANCINI WITH SLOW-COOKED TOMATO SAUCE

I wanted to take everything that's great about eggplant parmesan, one of my favorite dishes, and make it lighter and more compact and arancini seemed to be a good way to pull this off. This recipe takes some time to prepare, but once you've made the rice balls, they can be frozen and fried any time, which makes them great for parties (just make a few batches ahead of time). The tomato sauce will keep in the refrigerator for a few days, too.

Makes 4 servings

Preheat the oven to 450°F.

Place the whole eggplant on a baking sheet and coat with 2 tablespoons olive oil. Season to taste with salt and pepper and bake until the inside of the eggplant is soft and the outside is charred, about 25 to 30 minutes. Remove from the oven and, when cool enough to handle, remove and discard the skin. Cut the eggplant flesh into ½-inch pieces, then place in a colander to drain.

Transfer the drained eggplant to a bowl and add half of the garlic, basil, half of the Parmesan, the red pepper flakes, and 2 tablespoons breadcrumbs. Mix well, then season to taste with salt and pepper and set aside.

In a medium saucepan, heat the remaining olive oil over medium heat. Add the Arborio rice and cook, stirring, until lightly toasted, about 2 minutes. Add the shallot and the remaining garlic and cook, stirring, for 1 minute. Add the beer and simmer until the liquid has been absorbed, about 2 to 3 minutes. Add half of the vegetable stock and cook, stirring frequently. Continue adding the remaining stock, a little at a time, until the rice is tender, but still thick and starchy, about 20 minutes. Turn off the heat and stir in the remaining Parmesan. Let cool to room temperature.

In a shallow bowl, whisk together the eggs and water. Place the flour in another bowl and season with salt and pepper. Add the remaining breadcrumbs to a third bowl. Take 3 tablespoons of the cooled risotto and form it into disk. Place 1 tablespoon of eggplant mixture in the middle of the disk and form the rice around it into a ball. Roll the rice ball in the flour until lightly coated all over. Dredge the ball in the egg

1 large eggplant, about 1½ pounds

¼ cup olive oil

Kosher salt

Freshly ground black pepper

2 garlic cloves, thinly sliced

8 large basil leaves, finely chopped

½ cup grated Parmesan cheese

¼ teaspoon red pepper flakes

1 cup fresh breadcrumbs

1 cup Arborio rice

½ cup finely chopped shallot

¼ cup beer, preferably a blonde ale

3 cups vegetable stock or water

2 large eggs

2 tablespoons water

All-purpose flour

Vegetable oil, for frying

Slow-Cooked Tomato Sauce, for serving (recipe follows)

PAIRING STRATEGY

Salty, crispy fried foods, like arancini, will go with just about any beer, but brightly acidic tomatoes really pop with a super crisp kölsch or pilsner.

RECOMMENDED BEERS

STS Pils, Russian River Brewing Company
Kölsch, Prost Brewing Company
Polestar Pilsner, Left Hand Brewing Company
Octoberfest, Bell's Brewery

mixture, letting the excess drip off, then coat the ball in breadcrumbs. Transfer to a platter and repeat with the remaining rice. (At this point, the arancini can be frozen, if you want to use them at a later date.)

Add enough vegetable oil to a large, heavy saucepan to completely submerge the arancini, and then heat the oil until an inserted instant-read thermometer reads 350°F. Working in batches of four at a time, carefully place the arancini in the oil, and fry until they're crispy and deep golden brown, about 2 to 2½ minutes. Using a slotted spoon, transfer to a paper towel–lined baking sheet and repeat with the remaining arancini.

Serve the arancini immediately with warm tomato sauce on the side for dipping.

SLOW-COOKED TOMATO SAUCE

Makes 2 cups

¼ cup olive oil

2 pounds Early Girl tomatoes (San Marzanos or Roma tomatoes are a good alternative), cored and quartered

2 garlic cloves, thinly sliced

1 shallot, thinly sliced

2 teaspoons red pepper flakes

¼ cup basil leaves, torn (about 2 ounces)

Kosher salt

Freshly ground black pepper

Heat the oil in a large saucepan or Dutch oven over medium heat. Add the tomatoes and cook, stirring often, for 5 minutes. Add the garlic, shallot, red pepper, and basil, and season with salt and black pepper. Reduce the heat to low, cover the pot and simmer until a slightly deeper red hue becomes apparent, and the sauce coats the back of a spoon; 30 to 40 minutes. Remove from the heat and transfer to a food processor; pulse until smooth. Season to taste with salt and pepper. Refrigerate until ready to use, up to three days.

GRILLED CORN, FENNEL, AND ARUGULA SALAD WITH PARMESAN VINAIGRETTE

I'm one of those fennel advocates who believes it's often overlooked and widely underused. It's so versatile and I like it both melted over heat in olive oil, as well as a raw, crunchy component in salads. For this summery dish, I match it up with peppery arugula to balance out the sweet corn and salty, nutty Parmesan. This is a great warm weather entrée salad, but it can also be a good side for grilled fish or chicken.

Makes 4 entrée-size servings or 6 appetizer servings

Prepare a medium-hot charcoal or gas grill.

In a large bowl, add the fennel, olive oil, lemon juice, and lemon zest. Season with salt and pepper and toss well.

Place the corn on the grill grates and close the cover. Roast for about 10 minutes; the husks will blacken. Transfer to a plate and, when cool enough to handle, shuck the corn. Cut the kernels from the cobs into the bowl with the fennel; toss well and season to taste with salt and pepper. Add the arugula, mint, and half each of the parsley, chives, and dill.

Divide the salad among plates or serve on a platter. Garnish with the remaining parsley, chives, dill, and the reserved fennel fronds. Spoon some of the Parmesan Vinaigrette over the salad. Finish with a crank of black pepper and serve immediately.

2 large fennel bulbs, halved, cored, and thinly sliced with a sharp knife or mandoline between $1/4$- and $1/8$-inch-thick, fronds reserved

2 tablespoons extra-virgin olive oil

Finely grated zest and juice of 2 lemons

Kosher salt

Freshly ground black pepper

4 ears of corn in the husk, tough leaves and tassels removed

6 cups arugula

2 sprigs mint, torn

1 cup parsley leaves, loosely packed

$1/4$ cup thinly sliced chives

$1/4$ cup dill fronds

Parmesan Vinaigrette (recipe follows)

PAIRING STRATEGY

I've always found that the natural sweetness of corn has the unique ability to push the flavors of malt and hops together. Normally when you taste a beer, they're very separate from one another, but here the grilled corn is a bridge. As an added bonus, fennel quietly accents the hops, making them a bit more pronounced.

RECOMMENDED BEERS

Helles Belles, Ninkasi Brewing
UFO White, Harpoon Brewery
Allagash White, Allagash Brewing Company

PARMESAN VINAIGRETTE

Makes 1 cup

Place all ingredients in a blender or food processor and pulse until well combined. Refrigerate until ready to use, up to two days.

½ cup finely grated Parmesan cheese

½ cup extra-virgin olive oil

2 teaspoons finely grated lemon zest

3 tablespoons fresh lemon juice

2 garlic cloves

2 teaspoons freshly ground black pepper

½ teaspoon kosher salt

¼ cup basil leaves

DUNGENESS CRAB WITH AVOCADO AND GRAPEFRUIT

This dish is best done when Dungeness crab is in season, which was usually near Thanksgiving during my time in San Francisco. East coasters can sub in blue crab, but note that on either coast, the sweetness of the meat is usually in contrast to the saltiness of the water where it was caught. Though picking the meat is a laborious process (sometimes you can buy it pre-cleaned), I like the challenge, and it makes the dish taste better.

Makes 4 servings

Finely zest one grapefruit and set the zest aside. Use a knife to peel the grapefruits, removing all of the white pith. Working over a bowl to catch the juices, carefully cut between the grapefruit membranes to separate segments. When all segments suprêmes are removed, set them aside and squeeze the leftover membranes and pulp to extract as much juice as possible, removing any seeds. Add the reserved zest, honey, and olive oil to the bowl and whisk to combine. Season to taste with salt and pepper.

In a bowl, combine the crab with 2 tablespoons of the grapefruit dressing and set aside.

In a medium bowl, toss the arugula, radishes, avocado, parsley leaves, and tarragon and season with salt and pepper. Dress the greens until lightly coated and divide among four plates.

Divide the salad among plates. Top the salads with the crab and grapefruit suprêmes. Spoon 1 tablespoon of dressing over each plate and serve immediately.

3 ruby red grapefruits

1 tablespoon honey

2 tablespoons olive oil

Kosher salt

Freshly ground black pepper

½ pound Dungeness lump crabmeat, picked over for shells

2 cups (about 3 ounces) baby arugula or spicy greens

4 baby radishes or French Breakfast radishes, thinly sliced

2 ripe avocados, pitted and cut into thin wedges

¼ cup parsley leaves, torn

2 tablespoons tarragon, coarsely chopped

PAIRING STRATEGY
Crab brings salinity, avocado balances that with fat, and grapefruit adds acidity, all in equal portions, similar to the build of these beers; hops (for salt), carbonation (for fat), and an ABV level that's similar to the acidity of grapefruit. It's about balance.

RECOMMENDED BEERS
5 O'Clock Pils, Saint Arnold Brewing Company
Nomad, Great Divide Brewing Company
Colorado Kölsch, Steamworks Brewing Company

GRILLED CLAMS WITH SPICY CORN AND GARLIC AIOLI

All too often, really good quality clams are boiled or steamed with liquids (beer even!) that mask their true flavor. I say just grill them and let their salty creaminess stand on its own. This recipe captures all of the briny juice released from the clams while cooking and puts it to use as a base for a buttery, spicy sauce for the clams that gets tossed in at the end. The deal is sealed with a garlicky aioli, as all the best things are.

Makes 4 to 6 servings

In a small bowl, combine the butter, garlic, serrano peppers, and lemon juice. Blend with a fork until well mixed and set aside.

Prepare a hot charcoal or gas grill.

In a medium skillet, heat the olive oil over medium heat. Add the corn and cook, stirring frequently, until lightly browned, about 2 to 3 minutes. Stir in the paprika, remove from the heat, and let cool slightly. Add half of the butter mixture to the pan and stir until the corn is well coated in the sauce. Set aside.

Place the clams directly on the grill grates and cover the grill. Grill the clams, transferring them to the skillet with the corn as they open, about 5 to 7 minutes (discard any clams that do not open after 8 minutes). Add the remaining butter to the corn and stir to mix with the juices from the clams. Season to taste with salt and pepper.

Place the corn mixture on plates or a platter. Dot each clam with aioli, garnish with parsley, and serve.

½ cup (1 stick) unsalted butter, at room temperature

2 garlic cloves, sliced

2 serrano peppers, seeded and thinly sliced

Juice of 1 lemon

2 tablespoons olive oil

4 ears of corn, kernels removed from the cob

1 tablespoon Spanish or hot paprika

36 littleneck clams, scrubbed

Kosher salt

Freshly ground black pepper

Garlic Aioli (recipe follows)

½ cup parsley leaves, for garnish

PAIRING STRATEGY

Once you crack open a cold beer with this dish, it will transport you to a beachside cookout. The beer will calm the heat of the peppers, so you can taste the flavor of spicy food, have a sip of beer, and not burn out your palate.

RECOMMENDED BEERS

Pivo Pils, Firestone Walker Brewing Company
Samuel Adams Noble Pils, The Boston Beer Company
Doble Buho, Odell Brewing Co.

GARLIC AIOLI

Makes ¾ cup

In a bowl, combine the yolks, lemon juice, and garlic. Whisking slowly and constantly, slowly add the canola oil. Once the canola oil is gone and the aioli is emulsified, slowly whisk in the olive oil and season to taste with salt. Refrigerate until ready to use, up to 10 days.

2 large egg yolks

Juice of 1 lemon

2 garlic cloves, finely chopped

½ cup canola oil

2 tablespoons olive oil

Kosher salt

GRILLED SALMON WITH HEIRLOOM TOMATOES, FRIED MUSHROOMS, AND ROUILLE

I have yet to catch an elusive king salmon; I'm 0 for 6, but when I get that elusive catch (aka Chinook), I'll very likely cook this dish. Freshwater salmon is more subtle in flavor than salmon caught in the North Atlantic, like the Pacific Coho or Sockeye Salmon, so it needs a few supporting ingredients to enhance its overall flavor. Salmon should be simply seasoned, grilled to medium doneness, and not overcooked. You're aiming for an equilibrium of moisture and fat to tie this whole dish together, fortified by the umami of tomatoes and mushrooms.

Makes 4 servings

In a small bowl, whisk together the olive oil, vinegar, garlic, onion, capers, and basil. Season to taste with salt and pepper and set aside.

Place the tomatoes in a bowl and cover with the olive oil mixture. Refrigerate until ready to use, or keep at room temperature if eating within the hour.

In a medium bowl, combine the flour, cornstarch, and baking powder. Whisk in the water until just smooth.

Add 3 inches of canola oil to a tall-sided saucepan and heat the oil until an inserted instant-read thermometer reads 350°F. Working in batches, dredge the mushrooms in the batter, letting the excess drip off. Gently place the mushrooms in the hot oil and fry until they're golden brown, 2 to 3 minutes. Transfer to a paper towel–lined plate and let drain while you repeat with the remaining mushrooms.

Prepare a hot charcoal or gas grill. Brush the salmon lightly with some of the oil from the tomato mixture. Season with salt and pepper and grill, turning once, until just cooked through, about 4 to 5 minutes per side. Transfer to a plate.

Divide the tomatoes among four plates. Divide the salmon among the plates and spoon the mushrooms around the salmon. Drizzle the remaining dressing over the salmon and serve immediately, with the rouille on the side.

2 tablespoons olive oil

2 tablespoons white balsamic vinegar

1 garlic clove, thinly sliced

¼ cup red onion, thinly sliced

2 tablespoons capers, drained

½ cups basil leaves, torn

Kosher salt

Freshly ground black pepper

2 pounds mixed heirloom tomatoes, cored and cut into ½-inch-thick wedges

1 cup all-purpose flour

1 cup cornstarch

1 teaspoon baking powder

1 cup water

Canola oil, for frying

1 pound mixed fresh mushrooms (such as shiitake, cremini, or maitake), cleaned and cut in ¾-inch pieces

Four 6-ounce salmon fillets, with skin

Rouille, for serving (recipe follows)

PAIRING STRATEGY

This dish has a lot going on, both in texture and flavor. The right beer will up the complexity even more, giving a hoppy herbal edge to the tomatoes, matching the umami of the mushrooms, and cutting through the rouille's richness.

RECOMMENDED BEERS

Tiny Bomb, Wiseacre Brewing
Rahr's Blonde, Rahr & Sons Brewing Company
Allagash White, Allagash Brewing Company

ROUILLE

Makes 1½ cups

Char the peppers over a gas grill or under a hot broiler until blackened all over. Transfer to a bowl, cover with plastic, and let steam for 20 minutes. Remove the cores, skins, and seeds from the peppers and tear the flesh into large pieces.

In a food processor, pulse the peppers, garlic, jalapeño, breadcrumbs, and 1 teaspoon salt until finely chopped. With the motor running, slowly add the oil, followed by the lemon juice and ½ teaspoon pepper, blending until very smooth. Refrigerate until ready to use, up to three days.

2 red bell peppers

6 garlic cloves

1 jalapeño, seeded and chopped

½ cup fresh breadcrumbs

Kosher salt

¾ cup extra-virgin olive oil

2 tablespoons fresh lemon juice

Freshly ground black pepper

OLIVE OIL–POACHED HALIBUT WITH FENNEL, GREEN OLIVES, AND LEMON

Halibut is very much a blank canvas when it comes to cooking—what you do with it will change its flavor and texture. Many cooks fry halibut, for fish and chips, but that really buries the gentle flavor of this fish. Poaching it gently in olive oil brings out its more delicate, fresh notes. Here, the olive oil is infused with fennel and citrus before adding the halibut, giving the dish a Mediterranean vibe that's made even stronger with herbs and green olives.

Makes 4 servings

Place the oil in a 5- to 6-quart heavy-bottomed pot and warm over medium heat until an inserted instant-read thermometer reads between 180° to 200°F (the oil should gently bubble). Season the oil with ¼ teaspoon each salt and pepper and add the garlic, fennel wedges, fennel seeds, sugar, bay leaf, and orange and lemon zests. Gently simmer until the fennel is tender, about 30 minutes. Using a slotted spoon, transfer the fennel, garlic, bay leaf, and zest to a bowl.

Return the oil to 180° to 200°F. Season the halibut with salt, add to the oil, and cook on one side only until opaque, 7 to 10 minutes. Carefully transfer the fish to a plate, cover with parchment, and let rest for 5 minutes.

Reheat the fennel mixture in a skillet over low heat, then discard the bay leaf.

Divide the vegetables and halibut among 4 plates. In a bowl, mix the chopped herbs, olives, and lemon juice with ¼ cup of the poaching oil. Spoon over the top of the fish and vegetables. Garnish with the fennel fronds and serve.

4 cups olive oil

Kosher salt

Freshly ground black pepper

8 garlic cloves, smashed

3 fennel bulbs, halved, cored, and cut into ¼-inch-thick wedges, fronds reserved

1 teaspoon fennel seeds

1 teaspoon granulated sugar

1 bay leaf

Strips of zest from 1 orange

Strips of zest and juice from 2 lemons

Four 6-ounce skinless halibut fillets, about 1½ to 2 inches thick

2 tablespoons finely chopped chives

2 tablespoons finely chopped parsley or chervil

2 tablespoons finely chopped tarragon

½ cup Castelvetrano olives, pitted and halved

PAIRING STRATEGY

The citrus, herbs, and fennel in this dish will pair up with various hops in different ways. While Citra, Chinook, and Centennial are citrusy hops, Simcoe, Saaz, and Tahoma are earthier and piney and will highlight distinct aspects of the dish. Play around with the pairings to see what you like best.

RECOMMENDED BEERS

Brooklyn Sorachi Ace, Brooklyn Brewery
Turntable Pils, Great Lakes Brewing Company
Schlafly White Lager, The Schlafly Tap Room

KEN GROSSMAN

SIERRA NEVADA BREWING CO.

It wouldn't be wrong to call Sierra Nevada's Ken Grossman a traditionalist; he's well aware of the late 1970s, where other than Anchor Brewing in San Francisco, there were only a handful of American breweries. They all made a similar mild-tasting lager because beer was believed to be simple and easy rather than complex and challenging. Of course, that meant the culinary world didn't really see a place for it. In the mid 1980s, Sierra Nevada had a product that they felt confident in, but their widespread acceptance and popularity wasn't until the 1990s. Chez Panisse, a Mecca for the farm-to-table movement, became Sierra Nevada's first key customer and helped establish it in the food scene. Now pale ales and IPAs are many people's starting point, whereas back then they seemed unapproachable. Those styles of beers used to be just about the bitterness, but now include an array of hops to create specific flavor profiles. Misperceptions about dark beer being "heavy" and high in alcohol have been overcome with education.

ON DRAFT

SIERRA NEVADA PALE ALE

This beer is iconic, balanced, and known for consistency and quality. It was one of the first hop-forward beers that broke into the market in the 1980s, and Ken was one of the only brewers around that used exclusively whole cone hops, not pellets. It's a true grilling beer: it connects with char and bridges hops and bitterness. It's great with salmon, asparagus, onions, halibut, chicken, and steak, though it can work surprisingly well with vinaigrettes in salads, too!

CHAPTER 02

HOPPY & BITTER

This is a misunderstood beer style. Many people have their first bad beer experience drinking one of these beers, simply because they don't understand what to expect from bitter hops. While this has been the strongest beer category in the United States for the past ten years, I believe it's beer and food pairings that have brought people back to this style even after swearing off it. How bitter a beer you enjoy is a matter of personal preference, but using food to complement the floral and citrus notes of the hops helps turn the bitterness into something more enjoyable.

A solid malt base balances the bitterness of good hop-forward craft beers. Because hop varieties are so widely varied, these beers cover a wide range of flavors: citrus (Cascade), pineapple (Centennial, Chinook, Amarillo), pine (Simcoe), and tropical fruits (Nelson Sauvin). These are bright beers that work as palate cleansers.

Hoppy beers with little or no malt structure can clash with some seafood, imparting a metallic flavor. Malt-forward beers with hops like ambers and some barley wines, have a bit more caramelization to them and pair well with earthy mushrooms and fatty meats. Assertive styles like fresh hops and imperial IPAs, which are intensely flavorful, can be upwards of 100 International Bittering Units (IBU), past the point at which most people can perceive bitterness. Some of these beers can certainly overpower dishes, but the fattier the food, the better for these intense hop profiles.

These beers are piney, deeply citrusy, herbal, and floral. They work with foods that need a bit of competition on the palate; think spicy, fatty, acidic. Anything that could use a little bitterness to offset a powerful flavor falls into this category. The hops do here what carbonation does in a lighter style, taking over the duty of cleansing the palate of any overwhelming and intense flavors.

SOME HOPPY & BITTER BEER STYLES

Amber

Barley Wine

ESB

Fresh Hop

Imperial IPA

IPA

Pale Ale

HOPPY & BITTER
FOOD FRIENDS

Aioli, bacon, bitter greens, carrot, chile peppers, chives, cream, cumin, fried chicken, garlic, parsley, sage, strong cheese (e.g. aged Gruyère, blue cheese), sweet potato, watercress

FOUR-CARROT SALAD WITH TOASTED GRAINS

Up at Sierra Nevada Brewing Co. in Chico, California, there's an incredible two-acre farm where they grow dozens of varieties of carrots, from tender and sweet to earthy and crunchy. When I don't have access to those, I search out the freshest, right-out-of-the-ground carrots I can get. I won't lie; this is not a quick and easy salad. But carrots are one of my favorite vegetables year-round—it's amazing how the four different forms that this humble ingredient takes on in this recipe affect the flavor and demonstrate the range of what a carrot can do.

Makes 4 servings

Make the confit carrots: Preheat the oven to 300°F. Place the carrots in a casserole or saucepan and cover with the olive oil. Add the coriander seeds and ¼ teaspoon each of salt and pepper. Cover tightly with foil, transfer to the oven, and braise until the carrots are soft all the way through when pierced with a fork, about 1 hour. Remove the carrots from the oven, uncover, and let cool to room temperature.

Make the marinated carrots: In a bowl, combine the carrot strips, sliced fennel, mustard, honey, fennel seeds, cumin seeds, and lemon juice. Season with salt and pepper and toss well to combine. Let marinate at room temperature for 1 hour, or cover and refrigerate overnight.

Make the pickled carrots: In a small saucepan, combine the red pepper flakes, champagne vinegar, water, and the pickling spices and bring to a boil. Place the carrots in a pint jar and top with the hot brine. Let sit at room temperature for 30 minutes, then cover and refrigerate overnight or for up to 36 hours.

Preheat the oven to 325°F and line a rimmed baking sheet with foil.

CONFIT CARROTS

1 bunch baby carrots, peeled and tops trimmed to ¼ inch

1 cup olive oil, more for drizzling

1 teaspoon coriander seeds

Kosher salt

Freshly ground black pepper

MARINATED CARROTS

4 large yellow carrots, peeled into long strips

1 fennel bulb, cored and very thinly sliced, fronds reserved

1 teaspoon whole-grain mustard

1 teaspoon honey

1 teaspoon fennel seeds, lightly toasted

1 teaspoon cumin seeds, lightly toasted

3 tablespoons fresh lemon juice

PICKLED CARROTS

1 teaspoon red pepper flakes

½ cup champagne vinegar

1 cup water

1 teaspoon pickling spice

1 bunch multicolored baby carrots, peeled, tops trimmed to ¼ inch, and cut into rounds or spears

---

PAIRING STRATEGY

Carrots can be quite pronounced with their sweetness, even in this recipe where there are so many textures, flavors, and spices used. Look for a beer that will break up that uniformity with hoppy boldness.

RECOMMENDED BEERS

Pale Ale, Sierra Nevada Brewing Co.
Anvil ESB, AleSmith Brewing Company
TexiCali Nut Brown Ale, Freetail Brewing Company

Complete the dish: Transfer the quinoa to the prepared baking sheet and toss with the olive oil. Bake the quinoa until lightly toasted, 12 to 15 minutes. Remove from the oven and set aside. Divide the confit carrots among four plates. Layer on the marinated, pickled, and raw carrots and gently mix. Spoon the quinoa over the carrots and top with the pistachios, fennel fronds, and a drizzle of olive oil.

TO COMPLETE

1½ cups cooked quinoa

2 tablespoons olive oil, plus more for finishing

3 medium carrots, peeled, then peeled again into long strips

¼ cup pistachios, toasted and chopped

BABY GREENS SALAD WITH CHÈVRE CROQUETTES AND HONEY BALSAMIC VINAIGRETTE

I prefer my cheese as an introduction to a meal, rather than a stand-alone dish at the end. Though these aren't cheese curds, which are delicious in their own right, using a goat cheese makes the fried coquettes much lighter so they're easily worked into a salad with lettuces of varying pepperiness and spiciness without overpowering them. The crispiness of the croquette adds a nice crunch too, and it's all rounded out by a sweet and sour salad dressing.

Makes 4 servings

In a shallow bowl, beat the eggs and milk together. Place the flour in another bowl, and the breadcrumbs in a third.

Gently form the cheese into logs that are about 1 inch long and ½ inch in diameter (they should resemble small marshmallows).

Coat a piece of cheese in the flour, then dredge in the egg mixture, letting the excess drip off. Coat the cheese in breadcrumbs, making sure to completely cover it. Transfer to a parchment-lined plate and repeat with the remaining cheese. Refrigerate the croquettes while you prepare the rest of the salad.

In a bowl, whisk together the honey, vinegar, mustard, and olive oil. Season to taste with salt and black pepper. Pour the vinaigrette over the tomatoes and let them marinate for 10 minutes. Add the sliced cucumber to the tomato and balsamic mixture, toss well, and set aside.

Heat the canola oil in a skillet over medium heat. Working in batches, fry the croquettes until golden brown on all sides, about 2 to 3 minutes. Using a slotted spoon, transfer the croquettes to a paper towel–lined baking sheet and repeat until all of the croquettes have been fried. Season with salt.

Place the greens in a medium bowl and spoon some of the liquid from the tomato-cucumber mixture over top. Toss the greens well and gently distribute among four plates, seasoning with a crank of black pepper. Dole out the tomatoes and cucumbers and place the croquettes on top of the salad. Garnish with the herbs and serve.

2 large eggs

¼ cup whole milk

½ cup all-purpose flour

½ cup fresh breadcrumbs, pulsed fine in a food processor

8 ounces firm chèvre (fresh goat cheese)

2 tablespoons honey, look for a floral wildflower variety

2 tablespoons balsamic vinegar

¼ teaspoon Dijon mustard

¼ cup olive oil

Kosher salt

Freshly ground black pepper

1 cup small tomatoes (such as pear or Sweet 100s), quartered

3 Persian cucumbers, thinly sliced

½ cup canola oil

4 cups mixed baby greens

1 cup loosely packed herbs, such as fennel fronds, parsley, and chives

PAIRING STRATEGY

No one ever thinks to match beer with salads, but it's sort of a no-brainer—green things are fantastic with hops. With this salad in particular, a fragrant, hoppy beer nicely amplifies the bitterness of the baby greens and the floral quality of honey.

RECOMMENDED BEERS

Edward, Hill Farmstead Brewery
Boomsauce, Lord Hobo Brewing Company
Samuel Adams Nitro IPA, Boston Beer Company

SAUTÉED CHANTERELLE MUSHROOMS WITH ROASTED FENNEL AND CRISPY ONIONS

Chanterelles are Mother Nature's golden nuggets; not only are they golden in color, but golden in taste, and sometimes in price too. But they're always worth it. When they're in season, I see no reason not to eat this as a decadent vegetarian entrée; the fried onions and fennel bring out this favorite fungi's inherent sweetness. Or share with friends and serve it as an appetizer.

Makes 4 to 6 servings

Preheat the oven to 375°F.

In a bowl, toss the onion with salt and let stand for 20 minutes while preparing the fennel.

In a bowl, toss the fennel wedges with the olive oil and season with salt and pepper. Line a rimmed baking sheet with foil and arrange the fennel on top. Roast until lightly browned, 20 to 25 minutes.

While the fennel is roasting, heat the canola oil in a saucepan until an inserted instant-read thermometer reads 250°F.

Toss the onion with the flour and season generously with salt and pepper. Working in batches, fry the onions, stirring to separate the rings, until crispy and golden brown, 2 to 3 minutes. Transfer to a paper towel–lined plate.

Melt the butter in a medium skillet and heat until it just begins to brown. Add the chanterelles and season with salt and pepper. Cook the mushrooms without stirring until they begin to brown, then stir and continue cooking until browned and crispy around the edges, 5 to 7 minutes total. Add the garlic and cook for 1 minute. Add the sherry vinegar, tarragon, chives, and parsley. Stir to combine and turn off the heat.

Arrange the fennel on a large plate and top with the chanterelles and fried onions. Spoon any liquid from the mushrooms over the top. Garnish with the fennel fronds and serve.

1 medium sweet onion, thinly sliced

Kosher salt

2 medium bulbs fennel, cored and cut into six wedges each, fronds reserved for garnish

2 tablespoons olive oil

Freshly ground black pepper

2 cups canola oil

½ cup all-purpose flour

2 tablespoons unsalted butter

1½ pounds chanterelle mushrooms, cleaned and cut into bite-size pieces

2 garlic cloves, thinly sliced

1 tablespoon sherry vinegar

2 tablespoons coarsely chopped tarragon leaves

1 tablespoon finely chopped chives

¼ cup parsley leaves

PAIRING STRATEGY
Malt-forward beers with substantial hops will augment the earthiness of the mushrooms, while highlighting the tarragon and chives. The fennel matches well with Simcoe or other floral, herbaceous hops, which will boost the flavor of the alliums, too.

RECOMMENDED BEERS
60 Minute IPA, Dogfish Head Craft Brewery
Dobis, Cellarmaker Brewing Company
IPA, Crooked Stave Artisan Beer Project

RICOTTA GNOCCHI WITH PARMESAN BRODO

Gnocchi is one of my all-time favorite dishes to make: from mixing the dough, to rolling out pieces like little pillows, it's near therapeutic. Some swear by using purely potato, others incorporate semolina for crunch, but I like the delicate richness of ricotta gnocchi, made even better floated in Parmesan broth. For a little flash of green, I sauté peas with ramps and garlic scapes to help break up the cheesiness of the dish. The real trick here is to save all your Parmesan rinds in a resealable plastic bag in the freezer for just such an occasion.

Makes 4 servings

Make the gnocchi dough: In a bowl, combine the ricotta, egg, and Parmesan and mix until smooth. Using your hands or a fork, gently work in ½ cup of the flour until well mixed. Add another ¼ cup flour and continue to mix, then season with ½ teaspoon salt. If the dough is still sticky, add more flour, 1 tablespoon at a time, until you can roll the dough between your fingers without sticking.

Wrap the dough in plastic and let rest at room temperature for at least 30 minutes and up to 1 hour.

Make the gnocchi: Lightly coat a work surface with flour and scatter some flour in the bottom of a rimmed baking sheet. Take about ¼ cup of the dough and roll it between your hands to form a rope. Place the dough on the work surface and continue rolling with your hands until the rope is uniform and about ½-inch thick. Cut the dough into 1-inch pieces and transfer the gnocchi to the floured baking sheet. Repeat with the remaining dough. Place the baking sheet in the freezer for 30 minutes to 1 hour to set.

Make the brodo: In a saucepan, combine the Parmesan rind, carrot, onion, celery, and stock. Bring to a boil, then lower the heat and simmer for 1 hour. Pour the brodo through a fine-mesh strainer and discard the solids. The brodo can be made up to 24 hours ahead of time and refrigerated until ready to use.

Heat the oil and butter in a large skillet over medium-high heat until the butter has melted. Working in batches (don't crowd the pan), add the gnocchi and cook without moving the pan, until the gnocchi is browned on one side, about 30 seconds. Gently flip the gnocchi over and cook until the

FOR THE GNOCCHI

16 ounces ricotta cheese

1 large egg

1 cup grated Parmesan cheese

1 cup all-purpose flour, plus more as necessary

Kosher salt

FOR THE BRODO

1 Parmesan cheese rind, about 4 ounces

1 carrot, cut into thirds

1 medium onion, cut into quarters

1 celery stalk, cut into thirds

4 cups chicken or vegetable stock

TO COMPLETE

2 tablespoons olive oil

2 tablespoons unsalted butter

¼ cup garlic scapes, thinly sliced

¼ cup thinly sliced ramps (or spring onions)

Kosher salt

Freshly ground black pepper

1 cup shelled English peas (from about 1½ pounds unshelled pea pods)

2 ounces pea tendrils, for garnish

Grated Parmesan cheese, for serving

PAIRING STRATEGY
Any hop-forward beer with herbal notes will soften the boldness of the scapes and ramps, making room for the gentle flavors of the gnocchi and brodo.

RECOMMENDED BEERS
Bottle Rocket Pale Ale, Wormtown Brewery
Mini Boss, Eureka Heights Brewing Company
Citra Pale Ale, Upslope Brewing Company

other side is browned, about 30 seconds longer. Transfer to a plate and set aside. Repeat with the remaining gnocchi.

In the same pan, combine the garlic scapes and ramps and season to taste with salt and pepper. Cook the vegetables until softened, 2 to 3 minutes. Add the peas and enough brodo to fill the pan with 1 to 2 inches of liquid. Bring the liquid to a boil, then lower the heat and simmer the vegetables for

5 minutes, until tender. Add the gnocchi and simmer until warmed through. Season to taste with salt and pepper if needed.

Divide the gnocchi, vegetables, and brodo among four bowls. Garnish with the pea tendrils and grated Parmesan cheese and serve.

PRESSED CHICKEN WITH BRAISED BEANS AND PICKLED PEPPERS

It's not easy to render crispy chicken skin while also keeping the meat moist and juicy. For this recipe keep the chicken pressed in constant contact with the bottom of the pan for a consistent sear on the skin. This chicken is finished with a knob of butter and topped with a touch of pickling liquid to ensure this dish is always a part of the clean plate club.

Makes 4 servings

Preheat the oven to 325°F.

Place the peppers in a jar or other heatproof container. In a saucepan, bring the vinegar, water, sugar, and 2 tablespoons salt to a boil, then pour over the peppers. Let cool to room temperature, then refrigerate overnight.

In a casserole dish or heavy-bottomed pot, combine the beans, 5 cups of the stock, the onion, carrot, bay leaf, and olive oil. Cover the pot tightly with foil and bake in the oven until beans are tender but still firm, about 1½ hours. Season to taste with salt and pepper; discard the bay leaf. Turn the oven up to 375°F.

In a skillet, heat 2 tablespoons canola oil to high heat. Season the chicken with salt and pepper and place, skin side down, in the pan. Cook without moving until browned on one side, 3 to 5 minutes. Add the butter, thyme, and smashed garlic cloves. Set a cast-iron pan on top of the chicken. Transfer to the oven and roast until the chicken is cooked through, 20 to 25 minutes. Remove the chicken from the pan and transfer it to a platter, skin side up, discarding the thyme and garlic but leaving any remaining liquid in the pan. Add the kale to the pan along with the sliced garlic and chiles. Add the remaining stock and bring to a simmer. Cook until the kale is tender and the liquid has reduced to about ¼ cup, 15 to 20 minutes. Add the beans along with 2 tablespoons of the pepper pickling liquid. Simmer for a few minutes, until the liquid has thickened, then turn off the heat and stir in the parsley.

Divide the beans and kale among plates. Top with the chicken and a few slices of pickled pepper. Drizzle with some of the liquid from the skillet and serve.

6 mini sweet peppers, sliced into ⅛-inch rounds

1 cup distilled white vinegar

1 cup water

2 tablespoons granulated sugar

Kosher salt

2 cups dried cranberry or northern beans, soaked overnight and drained

6 cups chicken or vegetable stock

1 medium white onion, quartered

1 carrot, coarsely chopped

1 bay leaf

½ cup olive oil

Freshly ground black pepper

¼ cup canola oil

1 whole chicken, split in half with backbone and breastbone removed, each half with a breast, thigh, and leg

2 tablespoons unsalted butter

3 thyme sprigs

3 garlic cloves, 2 smashed and 1 thinly sliced

1 bunch Lacinato kale (aka Tuscan kale), torn into large pieces

2 Fresno chiles (or ¼ teaspoon red pepper flakes)

2 tablespoons chopped parsley

PAIRING STRATEGY

This is a classic hop situation where the bitterness of the beer breaks through the fattiness of the roasted chicken. A maltier beer will bring out the earthiness of the beans; a brighter one will amplify the pickled component.

RECOMMENDED BEERS

Zombie Dust, 3 Floyds Brewing Co.
West Sixth IPA, West Sixth Brewing
Dale's Pale Ale, Oskar Blues Brewery

SEARED SALMON WITH CARAWAY SPAETZLE AND CRÈME FRAÎCHE

You don't see enough spaetzle these days. It's a Germanic egg noodle that's surprisingly easy to make and has so many variations. Here, the crispy spaetzle acts as a substitute for crisped salmon skin. Add in soft, luscious crème fraîche and your fork will be swimming through the plate for a perfect bite of all three components together, a trifecta of bitterness, herbs, and fat.

Makes 4 servings

Bring a large pot of water to a boil and season with salt. Prepare an ice bath.

Meanwhile, in a large bowl, whisk together the milk, eggs, and rye flour until well blended. Add the all-purpose flour and, using your hands or a wooden spoon, mix until well combined and batter-like (the dough will be sticky). Season with a pinch of salt, add the caraway seeds, and stir to combine.

Using a spaetzle press or a colander with large holes, push the dough into the boiling water (it should form small dumplings). Boil the dumplings until they float, about 3 to 5 minutes. Using a slotted spoon or mesh strainer, transfer the spaetzle to the ice bath to cool briefly, then transfer to a paper towel–lined platter. When all of the spaetzle have been cooked, toss them with 1 tablespoon of the canola oil and reserve.

Heat a skillet over high heat. Pat the salmon dry and season with salt and pepper. Lower the heat to medium-high and add the remaining oil to the pan. Place the salmon in the pan; if it has skin, place it skin side down; if not, place the rounded side down. Cook until the salmon is browned on one side, then flip and continue cooking until the salmon is cooked through, about 5 to 7 minutes total. Transfer the salmon to a plate and let rest.

Melt the butter in a large skillet over high heat. When the foaming subsides, add the spaetzle and cook, tossing frequently, until lightly browned. Season to taste with salt and pepper.

Spoon some of the crème fraîche across the bottom of four plates and top with the spaetzle. Place the salmon on top of the spaetzle and garnish with the herbs. Serve immediately.

Kosher salt

¼ cup whole milk

2 large eggs, beaten

2 tablespoons rye flour

1 cup all-purpose flour

1 teaspoon caraway seeds, toasted and coarsely ground

3 tablespoons canola oil

Four 5-ounce salmon fillets

Freshly ground black pepper

2 tablespoons unsalted butter

½ cup crème fraîche

½ cup parsley leaves

½ cup dill fronds

6 chives, cut into 1-inch pieces

PAIRING STRATEGY

Hops elevate the herb garnish and help bring this dish together as one cohesive bite. The malt enhances the richness of the salmon, whereas the caraway aromatizes the dish like hops.

RECOMMENDED BEERS

The Pupil, Societe Brewing Company
Peeper Ale, Maine Brewing Company
Two Hearted Ale, Bell's Brewery

FRIED CHICKEN FOR VINNIE

For the last several years, my friend Vinnie Cilurzo, the owner and brewmaster of Russian River Brewing Company, and I have been cooking in pursuit of the ultimate fried chicken recipe. Our best rendition to date came from coating the chicken in baking powder and salt and allowing it to marinate in lemon juice in the fridge for a while before dredging and frying. This keeps the chicken tender and moist during the cooking process. We always abide by Vinnie's golden rule: the chicken has to be bone-in, if not, it's not fried chicken.

Makes 4 servings

In a large bowl, combine the baking powder and 2 teaspoons salt. Add the chicken pieces and coat well. Transfer to a large resealable plastic bag and add the lemon. Refrigerate for at least 12 hours and ideally 24 hours. Remove the lemon before the next step.

In a large bowl, toss the chicken with the buttermilk until well coated. Refrigerate for 1 hour.

In a shallow bowl, combine the paprika, garlic powder, oregano, black pepper, cayenne, flour, and cornstarch and mix well. In another bowl, beat the eggs with the milk and hot sauce. Remove one piece of chicken from the buttermilk and shake off any excess liquid. Dredge a piece of the chicken in the flour mixture, making sure it's well coated. Coat the chicken in the egg mixture, letting the excess drip off, then dredge again in the flour mixture. Transfer to rimmed baking sheet fitted with a wire rack and repeat with the remaining chicken.

Heat 2 inches of canola oil in a heavy-bottomed frying pan until an inserted instant-read thermometer reads 425°F. Preheat the oven to 325°F and line a rimmed baking sheet with foil.

Working in batches if necessary (don't crowd the pan), fry the chicken until golden brown and crispy on all sides; dark meat might take a minute or two longer than white. Transfer the chicken to the prepared baking sheet and season with salt. When all of the chicken is fried, transfer the baking sheet to the oven and bake until the internal temperature of the chicken reads 155°F on an instant-read thermometer. Let the chicken rest for 5 minutes before serving.

1 teaspoon baking powder

Kosher salt

1 whole chicken, separated into breasts, thighs, drumsticks, and wings

1 lemon, sliced into thin rounds

1½ cups buttermilk

2 tablespoons Spanish or hot paprika

1 teaspoon garlic powder

1 teaspoon dried oregano

2 tablespoons freshly ground black pepper

½ teaspoon cayenne pepper

1¼ cup all-purpose flour

½ cup cornstarch

2 large eggs

2 tablespoons whole milk

1 teaspoon hot sauce

Canola or peanut oil, for frying

PAIRING STRATEGY

Pale ales, IPAs, and ESBs are all great here; they're the all-time bests for washing down fried foods. But these beers can also play up the spices and dried herbs in the dry dredge, giving them a revived freshness.

RECOMMENDED BEERS

Pliny the Elder, Russian River Brewing Company
Interurban IPA, Fremont Brewing
Torpedo Extra IPA, Sierra Nevada Brewing Co.

THE ONLY BUTTERMILK BISCUIT RECIPE YOU'LL EVER NEED

Biscuits are great for breakfast, brunch, and barbecues, but a bad biscuit can ruin a whole meal. This one is fluffy and golden brown with the structural integrity to use for a sandwich, and the pillowy character required to sop up sauce. It's also an easy recipe to scale up, and with a little practice, this recipe will get stuck in your head, and you'll be able to go from bowl to oven in 5 minutes or less. I'm from the Midwest, where we wonder why people make round biscuits and have all those scraps? Roll it out and make squares, like the shape of most Midwestern states.

Makes about 10 biscuits

Preheat the oven to 425°F and line a baking sheet with parchment or a silicone baking mat.

In a large bowl, whisk together the flour, baking powder, salt, and sugar. Add the butter and use your fingertips to rub the chilled butter into the dry ingredients until the mixture resembles coarse meal. Add the buttermilk and stir just until the dough is evenly moistened.

Turn the dough out onto a cutting board and dust both sides of the dough with flour. Gently roll the dough out until it's about 2 inches thick. Using a knife or biscuit cutter, cut the dough into desired shapes (I like squares). Arrange the biscuits on the prepared baking sheet. Bake until golden brown and fluffy, 12 to 15 minutes.

Serve the biscuits warm with honey and softened butter.

3 cups all-purpose flour, plus more for dusting

1½ tablespoons baking powder

2 teaspoons kosher salt

2 tablespoons granulated sugar

⅔ cup cold unsalted butter (1 stick plus 3⅓ tablespoons), cut into small cubes

2 cups buttermilk

Honey and softened butter, for serving

PAIRING STRATEGY
The malt-build in Hoppy & Bitter beers actually helps bring out the butter and buttermilk flavor of these awesome biscuits. If you want to slather more butter on a freshly baked biscuit, these beers are here to support that notion.

RECOMMENDED BEERS
Summer Solstice, Anderson Valley Brewing
Mermaid's Red, Coronado Brewing Company
Flipside Red, Sierra Nevada Brewing Co.

PORK MEATBALLS WITH TOMATO SAUCE, BROCCOLI RABE, AND GRILLED SOURDOUGH

Any time I get a new cookbook, the first recipe I usually try is the meatballs; almost every food culture has its own version, so the meatballs are usually a good preview of that culture's flavor profiles. To make this truly Italian rendition, I use ricotta to keep the meatballs light and fluffy, cook them in San Marzano tomatoes for bright acidity, and serve them with broccoli rabe on the side to round out the meal. These make ridiculous next-day sandwiches, too, just add a little melted mozzarella.

Makes 4 servings

Preheat the oven to 450°F. Line two rimmed baking sheets with foil and brush the foil with ¼ cup of the olive oil.

In a large bowl, combine the pork, breadcrumbs, prosciutto, parsley, oregano, fennel seeds, ½ teaspoon of the red pepper flakes, the ricotta, and the eggs. Season the mixture with salt and pepper and mix with your hands until everything is well combined; the mixture should be a little bit wet to the touch. Add the basil and Parmesan and mix until blended. Form the mixture into 1- to 2-inch balls and transfer to the prepared baking sheet. Bake the meatballs until cooked through, about 15 minutes. Remove the meatballs from the oven and lower the temperature to 325°F.

In a food processor, blend the tomatoes until smooth and set aside.

Transfer the meatballs to a casserole dish. Add two of the sliced garlic cloves and the puréed tomatoes and toss to coat the meatballs. Cover tightly with foil and bake until cooked through and the sauce begins to thicken, 25 to 30 minutes. Remove from the oven and let rest, covered.

In a skillet, heat the remaining olive oil over medium-high heat. Add the broccoli rabe and cook, stirring often, for 1 to 2 minutes. Add the remaining garlic and red pepper flakes, and the chile and cook, stirring often, until the garlic begins to brown. Add the water, lower the heat, and cook until the broccoli rabe is crisp-tender, about 5 minutes. Transfer to a bowl and top with the shaved pecorino. Set aside.

¼ cup plus 2 tablespoons olive oil, plus more for brushing the bread

1¼ pounds ground pork, preferably from the shoulder

¼ cup fresh breadcrumbs

2 slices prosciutto, chopped into small pieces

1 cup chopped parsley leaves

1 teaspoon dried oregano

1 teaspoon fennel seeds

1 teaspoon red pepper flakes

½ cup ricotta cheese

2 large eggs

Kosher salt

Freshly ground black pepper

6 large basil leaves, chopped

2 tablespoons grated Parmesan cheese, plus more for garnish

One 28-ounce can diced tomatoes, preferably San Marzano

3 garlic cloves, thinly sliced

2 bunches broccoli rabe, trimmed

1 Fresno chile, thinly sliced

2 tablespoons water

¼ cup shaved pecorino cheese

Four thick-cut slices crusty sourdough or country bread

PAIRING STRATEGY
Hoppy & Bitter beers heighten the dried herbs in the meat mixture, bring lightness to the ricotta, and embrace the broccoli rabe's bitterness.

RECOMMENDED BEERS
AleSmith IPA, AleSmith Brewing Co.
The Great Return, Hardywood Park Craft Brewery
Modus Hoperandi, Ska Brewing Company

Heat a grill pan or skillet over high heat and brush the bread with olive oil. Toast the bread until golden brown on both sides.

Serve the meatballs in a large bowl with the bread, broccoli rabe, and any extra sauce on the side. Garnish the meatballs with extra Parmesan and serve.

CHICKEN THIGHS WITH CRISPY YUKON POTATOES AND BRAISED KALE

For some godforsaken reason, most restaurant menus feature chicken breasts more often than chicken thighs. I have no idea when and why this started, but thighs have much more flavor and moisture, which can result in an exponentially more delicious piece of meat. Most professional kitchens have a surplus of chicken thighs, which get relegated to staff meals. Even after all my years of working in restaurants, I'm still willing to make and eat this recipe any night of the week, even at home. So easy and satisfying, it's also great as leftovers and as a late-night second dinner.

Makes 4 to 6 servings

Preheat the oven to 375°F and line a rimmed baking sheet with foil.

In a bowl, season the chicken thighs with salt and pepper and toss with the thyme, sliced garlic, and ¼ cup of the canola oil. Transfer the chicken, skin side up, to the prepared baking sheet. Add half of the onions to the same bowl you used for the chicken and toss to coat. Scatter around the chicken and roast for 25 minutes. Add the carrots and continue roasting until the chicken is cooked through and vegetables are tender, about 10 minutes longer.

Heat the olive oil in a skillet over medium heat. Add the remaining onion and smashed garlic and cook, stirring frequently, for 2 to 3 minutes. Add the kale, red pepper flakes, and stock. Turn the heat to low, cover, and simmer until the kale is tender, about 30 minutes.

In another skillet, heat the remaining canola oil over medium-high heat. Add the potatoes and cook until golden brown, about 3 to 5 minutes each side.

Divide the kale among four plates and top with potatoes. Divide the chicken, onions, and carrots among the plates and spoon the remaining liquid from the kale over the plates.

6 bone-in, skin-on chicken thighs

Kosher salt

Freshly ground black pepper

1 teaspoon chopped thyme

4 garlic cloves, 2 sliced and 2 smashed

1¼ cups canola oil

1 medium sweet onion, cut into ¼-inch slices

1 bunch baby carrots, peeled and tops cut down to ½ inch

2 tablespoons olive oil

2 bunches kale, stems discarded, leaves torn into large pieces

1 teaspoon red pepper flakes

2 cups chicken or vegetable stock

2 pounds Yukon Gold potatoes, cut into 2-inch wedges (with skin)

PAIRING STRATEGY

Dark chicken meat and fried potatoes are heavier flavors, but a Hoppy & Bitter beer can break through and will lift up the herbal notes of the thyme and earthy notes of the vegetables. Look for a beer with more herbaceous hops (like Simcoe) or opt for a malty amber to bring out the caramelization of the meat.

RECOMMENDED BEERS

Daisy Cutter Pale Ale, Half Acre Beer Company
Automatic!, Creature Comforts Brewing Co.
Denver Pale Ale, Great Divide Brewing Company

THE TWO-BEER BURGER

For me, the perfect burger really starts with the meat. Buy the freshest ground beef you can find or grind your own. I like a brioche bun because they toast up nicely, setting the stage for you to customize your burger with whatever toppings and condiments you want. This burger is a true two-beer dish— drink one while you're cooking it, and another while eating it. I usually opt for a pale ale for prep and a brown ale at the table.

Makes 4 burgers

Preheat the oven to 400°F.

Line a small baking sheet with foil. Scatter the onion on the baking sheet, toss with the olive oil, and season with salt and pepper. Roast until softened and beginning to brown, about 20 minutes. Transfer the onions to a plate and set aside, leaving the foil in the baking sheet for cooking the bacon.

Place the mayonnaise in a small bowl. Whisk in the lemon juice. Season to taste with salt and pepper and refrigerate until ready to use.

In a small bowl, blend the brown sugar with the beer until well combined. Arrange the bacon on the baking sheet and brush with the beer and brown sugar mixture. Bake until crispy, about 15 minutes. Transfer to paper towels and set aside.

Prepare a hot charcoal or gas grill.

Divide the ground beef into 4 equal portions. Lightly take a portion in your hand and form it into a loose ball. Gently press the ball down to match the width of your buns. Run your palm around the edge of the patty to smooth the sides. Repeat with the remaining beef, and season the patties generously with salt and pepper.

Grill the burgers until well charred on one side. Flip the burgers and top with the cheese. Continue grilling until cooked to desired doneness, about 5 minutes per side for medium rare. When finished, transfer the burgers to a platter and let rest.

Meanwhile, lightly grill the buns. Spread the mayonnaise on both sides of the buns. Place the burgers on the dressed buns and top with onions and bacon. Serve with your favorite burger accoutrements.

1 medium yellow onion, thinly sliced

¼ cup olive oil

Kosher salt

Freshly ground black pepper

½ cup mayonnaise

1 teaspoon fresh lemon juice

2 tablespoons brown sugar

2 tablespoons beer, your choice (anything but Sour, Tart, & Funky)

4 slices thick-cut smoked bacon

1½ pounds ground sirloin or chuck, 80% to 85% lean

8 ounces shredded aged white Cheddar or dry jack

4 brioche buns, split

Whole-grain mustard

Ketchup (if you must)

PAIRING STRATEGY
Burgers are best while having a beer; hoppy beers refresh the palate, while dark roasty ones will match the richness of the meat.

RECOMMENDED BEERS

Pale Ale, Sierra Nevada Brewing Co.
Third-Eye Pale Ale, Steamworks Brewing Company
Indian Brown Ale, Dogfish Head Craft Brewery
Ellie's Brown Ale, Avery Brewing Co.
Blind Pig IPA, Russian River Brewing Company
Heady Topper, The Alchemist

BRAISED PORK SHOULDER IN ADOBO WITH PICKLED VEGETABLES

After growing up in the Midwest, where thick and sticky barbecue sauce coats all braised and pulled pork, it was refreshing to learn this less cloying, more umami-driven recipe from chef Carlo Lamagna at Clyde Common in Portland, Oregon. Tangy adobo is a big flavor, and the pickled vegetables that accompany this dish are used to bring out the vinegar and add some texture to each bite. This dish, inspired by Carlo's Filipino heritage, is best served family style right out of the Dutch oven with plenty of jasmine rice to go with it.

Makes 4 to 6 servings

In a medium saucepan, bring the rice vinegar, the water, sliced garlic, 1 teaspoon salt, and the sugar to a boil. Place the cauliflower, onion, chile, and carrot in a heatproof bowl and pour the hot liquid over. Let cool to room temperature, then cover and chill for at least 2 hours or overnight.

In a large bowl, combine the pork, smashed garlic, bay leaves, peppercorns, and soy sauce. Let rest at room temperature for 10 to 15 minutes.

Heat the oil in a Dutch oven or large saucepan over high heat. Working in batches if necessary (don't overcrowd the pan), add the pork and any leftover marinade and brown on all sides. Transfer to a plate and repeat until all the meat is seared, then return the pork to the Dutch oven and add the white vinegar and chicken stock. Cover the pot, lower the heat, and cook the pork at a gentle simmer, stirring every 20 minutes or so, until tender, 75 to 90 minutes. While braising, if the level of liquid falls below half the height of the meat, add more stock or water. If the liquid level is too high, uncover the pot and allow some to reduce. Remove from the heat and let rest for 10 to 15 minutes.

Use two forks to shred the pork into large chunks. Divide the rice among plates or bowls, top with the pork and some of the braising liquid, and serve with the pickled vegetables.

1 cup rice vinegar

2 cups water

10 garlic cloves, 2 sliced and 8 smashed

Kosher salt

1 tablespoon granulated sugar

1 head cauliflower, cut into small florets

1 red onion, thinly sliced

1 Fresno chile, seeds removed, sliced (or 1/4 teaspoon red pepper flakes)

1 carrot, peeled and thinly sliced in rounds

2 to 3 pounds boneless pork shoulder, cut into 2-inch pieces

2 bay leaves

1 teaspoon black peppercorns

1/2 cup soy sauce

2 tablespoons canola oil

1/2 cup white vinegar

2 cups chicken stock or water

Steamed jasmine rice, for serving

PAIRING STRATEGY

The hops add some citrus, think Cascade hops, or Centennial, Chinook, or Amarillo for a bit of pineapple which adds a nice touch of tropical flavor. Either way, any beer with these hops in it will round out the vinegar base.

RECOMMENDED BEERS

Union Jack, Firestone Walker Brewing Company
Hop Nosh, Uinta Brewing
Peeper, Maine Beer Company

TAMALES WITH ANCHO PORK CARNITAS

During my time working in kitchens in San Francisco, I had a tradition of picking up tamales for the staff from a vendor on the corner of 19th and Valencia on my way to work several mornings a week. While I'll never be able to replicate the tamales made by someone who's been making them for a lifetime in the Mission District, this is my humble attempt. Making tamales is a great family activity, and they freeze well, too: just warm them in the oven before eating.

Makes 6 servings

Preheat the oven to 300°F.

In a bowl, combine the masa with 1⅓ cups of the stock or water and mix well. Cover and let rest for 10 to 15 minutes.

In a stand mixer fitted with the paddle attachment, combine ½ cup canola oil or lard with the baking powder and 1½ teaspoons salt. Beat at medium high speed until light and fluffy, about 3 minutes, then add the masa mixture, ½ cup at a time, and mix until blended. Add more water or stock until the mixture reaches a soft, spreadable texture (you'll use around 1 cup). Cover and refrigerate the tamale dough for at least 1 hour and up to 24 hours.

Heat the remaining canola (or lard) in a Dutch oven or large saucepan over medium heat. Season the pork with salt and pepper. Working in batches if necessary (don't crowd the pan), brown the pork on all sides. Transfer to a plate and set aside. Add the onion, garlic, and bay leaf to the pan and cook, stirring frequently, until the onion is translucent and the garlic is fragrant, about 2 to 3 minutes. Add the jalapeño, tomatoes, ancho chile, and the remaining chicken stock or water. Return the pork to the pan, cover tightly, and transfer to the oven. Braise until the pork is very tender, about 2½ hours.

Remove the pot from the oven and let cool for 10 minutes. Adjust the oven to 375°F.

Transfer the pork to a bowl, leaving the liquid in the pot, and shred with a fork. Pour the liquid into a blender (or use an immersion blender) and blend until smooth. Pour this back over the pork and set aside.

2 cups masa harina

4⅓ cups chicken stock, vegetable stock, or water

¾ cup canola oil or lard

1½ teaspoons baking powder

Kosher salt

2 pounds boneless pork shoulder, cut into 2- to 3-inch pieces

Freshly ground black pepper

1 medium onion, diced

4 garlic cloves, sliced

1 bay leaf

2 jalapeños, seeded

One 12-ounce can diced tomatoes, with their juices

1 ancho chile pepper

1 dozen dried corn husks (available at Latin markets), soaked in water for 20 minutes

Sliced radishes, for serving

PAIRING STRATEGY

Jalapeños and ancho peppers give the carnitas a big kick; a Hoppy & Bitter beer is necessary to stand up to the heat. Bitter hops are great for scrubbing the palate after tamales, too.

RECOMMENDED BEERS

Big Swell IPA, Maui Brewing Co.
Racer 5 IPA, Bear Republic Brewing Co.
Avery IPA, Avery Brewing Co.

Working with one corn husk at a time, scoop ¼ cup tamale dough into the middle of the husk and use a spatula to spread it into a rectangle about ¼-inch thick, leaving a border of husk around each side. Add ¼ cup of the carnitas and spread it down the center of the dough. Fold in the long sides of the husk and roll the tamal between your fingers so the carnitas are completely enclosed in the filling. If the husks are long, fold in the ends. Tie the tamal with a strip of husk and place, seam side down, in a large baking pan. Repeat with the remaining husks and filling.

Add ½ inch of boiling water to the baking pan and cover tightly with foil. Bake the tamales until the dough is firm and separates easily from the husk, 30 to 45 minutes.

Arrange the tamales on a platter and serve with the radishes.

CARROT CAKE

Have you ever tried carrot cake with an IPA? You should. The sweetness from the carrots blends in with the malt, and the cream cheese frosting tempers the hops on your palate. This is a pretty classic carrot cake recipe, but this is less about the cake itself and more about the pairing. That said, the better the carrots you use here, the better your cake will be. Out in Petaluma, California there's a farm called County Line that grows some incredible carrots. Don't buy supermarket carrots for this one, go to your farmers' market or farmstand and get some dirty ones.

Makes 1 cake

Preheat the oven to 350°F. Grease a 9-inch round cake pan with oil, then flour it. Shake off any excess flour. In a bowl, whisk together the eggs, 1/2 teaspoon vanilla, the oil, and yogurt until smooth. In another bowl, whisk together the flour, both sugars, baking powder, baking soda, and the spices. Fold the yogurt mixture into the flour mixture and stir until no lumps remain. Fold in the carrots. Pour the mixture into the greased cake pan and smooth the top. Bake in the center of the oven for 10 minutes, then lower the temperature to 325°F and bake until the cake is golden brown and a toothpick inserted in the center comes out clean, about 35 minutes. Tip the cake out and transfer to a wire rack and let cool to room temperature.

Make the frosting: In the bowl of a stand mixer fitted with the whisk attachment, combine the cream cheese, salt, confectioners' sugar, vanilla, and the beer. Whip at medium speed until light and smooth.

Using a serrated knife, cut the cake horizontally into two layers. Spread one-third of the frosting evenly on top of the bottom layer. Place the other layer on top and use the remaining frosting to cover the top and sides of the cake.

Cut the cake into slices and serve with pints of IPA.

FOR THE CAKE

3/4 cup canola or vegetable oil, plus more for greasing the pan

3 large eggs

1/2 teaspoon pure vanilla extract (or the scrapings of 1/2 vanilla pod)

3/4 cup plain Greek yogurt

12 ounces all-purpose flour, plus more for the pan

1 1/3 cups granulated sugar

1/4 cup brown sugar

1 teaspoon baking powder

1 teaspoon baking soda

1/4 teaspoon ground allspice

1/4 teaspoon ground cinnamon

1/4 teaspoon ground nutmeg

1 1/2 cups grated carrots

FOR THE FROSTING

12 ounces cream cheese, at room temperature

1/2 teaspoon kosher salt

1 3/4 cups confectioners' sugar

1 1/2 teaspoons pure vanilla extract (or the scrapings of 1 1/2 vanilla pods)

3 1/2 tablespoons IPA beer

PAIRING STRATEGY

Grab a few friends who don't like hops and put this carrot cake in front of them with the hoppiest IPA you can find. Then get ready to congratulate yourself on converting those hop haters.

RECOMMENDED BEERS

Blind Pig IPA, Russian River Brewing Company
Tricerahops Double IPA, Ninkasi Brewing Company
Icy Bay IPA, Alaskan Brewing Co.

SAM CALAGIONE

DOGFISH HEAD
CRAFT BREWERY

S am Calagione may be a household name now, but when Dogfish Head Craft Brewery started in 1995, it was the smallest commercial brewery in America. Their focus was to be the first brewery to make beers unbeholden to the reinheitsgebot (German Beer Purity Law). Calagione began using nontraditional and culinary ingredients (such as lobster and spirulina) in his beers, but back then, it wasn't considered cool to digress from tradition. They were looked on more as weirdos and heretics than pioneers. But, thankfully, there were enough beer evangelists who shared the love for flavor-forward beers. It was during 2008, during this country's economic downturn, that the intersection of indie craft beer and farm-to-table food became a trend. Beer was an affordable luxury. In 1995, Chicory Stout was one of Dogfish Head's three core beers—a Mexican beer with notes of coffee and licorice, scented with Simcoe and Warrior hops, built on pale, roasted oatmeal grains. But back then, it was hard getting people to try it. So Calagione would bring dark chocolate nonpareils with him to every beer tasting, and invite drinkers to try the beer in tandem. Calagione advises folks to try the food first, then the beer for a palate-clearing sip. He claims you need at least a few bites of the proverbial apple to appreciate the pairing of two components into one. Their Namaste White is a Belgian-style white ale brewed with dried orange and a bit of coriander and peppercorns. Sounds more like a chef's recipe, right? It's amazing with goat cheese and mozzarella, garlicky veggie dishes, and roasted chicken. Flesh & Blood is an IPA brewed with a bevy of real citrus including orange peel, lemon flesh, and blood orange juice that is superb with aged cheddar, jerk chicken, and ceviche. SeaQuench Ale is a mashup of three sessionable beer styles: kölsch, gose, and Berliner weisse. This hybrid has lime peel, black limes, and sea salt, a must with raw oysters. If the technology ever came about to float a raw oyster in a beer can, I wouldn't put it past Calagione to someday sell this complete meal in a can!

ON DRAFT

INDIAN BROWN ALE

One of the most underrated and underbrewed beer styles out there, it's the Pinot Noir of the beer world. Sam's is versatile and food-friendly, with a bit of hops, higher carbonization, and brewed with brown sugar for a touch of sweetness. A match for roast duck, Peking duck, duck cassoulet, game birds . . . see a poultry trend? In other words, great with fatty, richer proteins; it crosses over into salmon territory, too.

CHAPTER 03

MALTY & SWEET

These beers are all about playing with the Maillard reaction. As John Mallet, director of operations at Bell's Brewery has told me, "Malt is rightfully identified as the soul of beer. And malt flavor is the heart of that soul. If beer lacked the generous flavors developed during the kilning of malt, it would be a paltry and unbalanced beverage. The Maillard reaction is responsible for critical flavor contributions to some of my favorite foods. The essences of luxurious chocolate, crusty bread, rich coffee, and perfectly roasted meats all arise from a shared base of Maillard generated flavors." Mallet wrote *Malt: A Practical Guide from Field to Brewhouse*, so you should listen to him.

One of the deepest connections between beer and food is the act of roasting, from roasted malts to roasted meats. Malty & Sweet beers develop caramel flavors and toffee notes due to the roast. These beers are less about contrasting and more about complementing, taking base flavors and bolstering them. Caramelization of sugars brings a touch of sweetness, driving hops to the roof of the mouth, and leaving heavier flavors on the palate.

Notes of nuts, toffee, and dried fruit are found in these malt-driven beers. Full-bodied and dark, they often rely on their carbonation level to showcase the little hops they have. A lot of German-style beers fall in this category, like the dark wheats: dunkel and doppelbock. They're biscuity, like toasted bread. Match these beers with foods that mimic these flavors, which can best be thought of as "crispy and browned," in other words, the Maillard reaction. Some beers like Bière de Garde and Scotch ales, have a deeper copper hue and go well with foods that pair with orange wines and whiskeys. Think fall squashes, rye grains, warming spices, molasses, earthy mushrooms, and glazed meats.

These beers are toasty, bready, and warm. They have notes of caramel and toffee and work well with foods that showcase a savory aroma or taste—especially roasted, glazed, and braised, rich foods that need a little sweet touch to balance them out.

SOME MALTY & SWEET BEER STYLES

American Amber Lager

American Brown Ale

Belgian-Style Dubbel

Bière de Garde

Doppleback

Dunkel

Scotch Ale

80
ROASTED DELICATA SQUASH SOUP WITH RYE CROUTONS

82
MORTGAGE LIFTER BEANS WITH CARROT VINAIGRETTE AND BREADCRUMBS

84
MUSHROOMS ON TOAST WITH MALTED BACON AND MUSTARD GREENS

87
ROASTED GAME HENS WITH MUSHROOM PANZANELLA

88
PORK CHOPS WITH MASCARPONE POLENTA, BROWN ALE–GLAZED FIGS, AND COLLARD GREENS

90
TAGLIATELLE WITH OXTAIL AND TOMATO SUGO

92
PAN-ROASTED PORK LOIN WITH SQUASH AND SALSA VERDE

94
SMOKED BEEF BRISKET WITH ROSEMARY CONFIT POTATOES

96
PORK SHOULDER PASTRAMI

99
BUTTERSCOTCH BUDINO WITH BROWN ALE CARAMEL

101
GINGERBREAD AND MOLASSES COOKIES

MALTY & SWEET
FOOD FRIENDS

Anchovies, beans, beets, celery, figs, mushrooms, nutmeg, pancetta, paprika, shrimp, soy sauce, spinach, squash, rye bread, thyme

ROASTED DELICATA SQUASH SOUP WITH RYE CROUTONS

During early fall, which comes early in the Rocky Mountains, this is easily a once-a-month recipe at my house, best eaten on the couch in front of the fireplace. This smooth, toasty squash soup is the perfect one-pot meal. Roasting the squash brings out its butteriness, which means that you don't have to add an excess of cream, making this a relatively healthy version of something that can often be quite rich. I love to contrast the sweetness of delicata squash with the intensely sour rye bread croutons and the bite of fresh horseradish.

Makes 4 to 6 servings

Preheat the oven to 400°F and line a rimmed baking sheet with foil. In a bowl, toss the squash with ¼ cup of the olive oil and the honey, and season with salt and black pepper. Scatter the squash on the prepared baking sheet, and then roast until lightly browned in spots, 25 to 30 minutes. Remove from the oven and lower the temperature to 325°F.

In a saucepan, combine the squash, stock, and ginger. Bring to a simmer, cover, and cook for 15 minutes covered. Turn off the heat and stir in the cream.

Using an immersion blender, purée the soup until smooth. Season to taste with salt and pepper and keep warm over very low heat.

In a bowl, toss the rye cubes with the remaining olive oil and the horseradish, using your hands to gently work the horseradish into the bread. Scatter the bread on a rimmed baking sheet and bake until lightly toasted, 12 to 15 minutes.

Divide the soup among bowls. Garnish with the croutons and some freshly grated horseradish and serve.

3 pounds delicata squash, ends trimmed, halved, seeds removed, and cut into 2-inch pieces

½ cup olive oil

2 tablespoons honey

Kosher salt

Freshly ground black pepper

5 cups vegetable or chicken stock

1 teaspoon grated fresh ginger

¼ cup heavy cream

2 cups cubed rye bread (about 1-inch pieces)

2 tablespoons freshly grated horseradish, plus more for garnish

PAIRING STRATEGY

These beers reinforce the sweetness in the bread and the deep nutty notes of the roasted squash, tempering the horseradish.

RECOMMENDED BEERS

Pursuit of Hoppiness, Grand Teton Brewing Company
Alaskan Amber, Alaskan Brewing Co.
District Common, Atlas Brew Works

MORTGAGE LIFTER BEANS WITH CARROT VINAIGRETTE AND BREADCRUMBS

A while ago, I found myself geeking out about beans with my friend Kyle Mendenhall, chef of Arcana in Boulder, Colorado, and Sean Clark, chef at El Moro in Durango, Colorado. Kyle and I had just discovered local Mortgage Lifter beans. These legumes are meaty, creamy, nutty, and for beans they have a surprisingly savory taste. They were a revelation for us! Sean then chimed in, "Yeah, I've been using them for years . . . in fact I live by the farm where the original ones were grown." Clearly we were out of the loop. I don't like to do much beyond braising them and adding a little vinaigrette, so as to not detract from their greatness. If you can't find Mortgage Lifters (they are available online), Gigantes or Giant Aztecs will do just fine.

Makes 4 to 6 servings

In a bowl, combine the finely diced carrots, shallot, mustard, honey, and lemon juice and toss well. Season with salt and pepper and let rest at room temperature for 30 minutes, or cover and refrigerate overnight.

Preheat the oven to 325°F.

In a Dutch oven or large saucepan, combine the beans, water, stock, remaining carrot, onion, celery, bay leaf, and the ½ cup of olive oil. Cover the top with a layer of parchment, then a layer of foil, and then cover the pot. Transfer the dish to the oven and braise until the beans are tender but still hold their shape, about 90 minutes. Remove the pot from the oven and let the beans cool, covered, to room temperature, stirring every 10 minutes or so. Remove the bay leaf and large chunks of vegetables, then strain the beans and reserve any remaining braising liquid (note: the beans might soak it all up).

In a skillet, heat the remaining olive oil over medium-high heat. Add the breadcrumbs and cook, stirring frequently, until golden brown. Stir in the parsley and set aside.

Divide the beans among plates or bowls, spoon some of the carrot vinaigrette on top (or toss with the beans beforehand) and garnish with the toasted breadcrumbs and herbs. Drizzle with olive oil and serve.

2 medium carrots, finely diced, plus 1 medium carrot, cut into thirds

1 small shallot, finely chopped

½ teaspoon Dijon mustard

1 teaspoon honey

1 tablespoon fresh lemon juice

Kosher salt

Freshly ground black pepper

2 cups dried Mortgage Lifter beans, rinsed and picked over (Gigante or Giant Aztec beans are good alternatives)

4 cups room-temperature water

4 cups chicken or vegetable stock

1 onion, cut into quarters

2 celery stalks, cut into thirds

1 bay leaf

½ cup plus 1 tablespoon olive oil, plus more for serving

½ cup fresh breadcrumbs

2 tablespoons finely chopped parsley

1 cup assorted coarsely chopped herbs, such as dill, mint, chives, and thyme

---

PAIRING STRATEGY

The meaty earthiness of these beans aligns nicely with a malty beer and its carbonation helps to enliven the dish.

RECOMMENDED BEERS

Steam Engine Lager, Steamworks Brewing Company
Hop Common, Peekskill Brewery
Amber Ale, West Sixth Brewing

MUSHROOMS ON TOAST WITH MALTED BACON AND MUSTARD GREENS

Mushrooms on toast is my comfort food. I wait all year for morels to be in season; if I could, I'd make this recipe nearly every day. Their ability to hold their texture and shape and their unmistakably poignant flavor is nearly impossible to substitute. No one ever made a diet dish with morels. To make this one even more decadent, I not only add bacon, but a little bit of malt syrup, too, showing there's nothing to do but go richer.

Makes 4 servings

Preheat the oven to 375°F and line a rimmed baking sheet with foil.

Brush the bread with olive oil and season with salt and pepper. Arrange on the prepared baking sheet and bake until toasted, 10 to 13 minutes. Remove from the oven and set aside.

Brush away any dirt or particles from the morels. If they are extra dirty, rinse them in a colander, then let dry before cooking.

Place the bacon in a skillet and turn the heat to medium-high. Cook the bacon until golden brown on both sides, about 5 minutes. Transfer the bacon to a plate, leaving the fat in the pan. Brush the bacon with the malt syrup and cut each slice of bacon in half. Set aside.

Heat the bacon fat over medium heat and add the shallots and mustard greens. Cook, stirring frequently, until the shallots are soft and the greens have wilted, 4 to 5 minutes. Transfer to a plate and keep warm. Reheat the pan over medium heat and add all of the mushrooms. Cook, stirring occasionally, until the shiitake or cremini mushrooms are soft and the morels are golden brown, about 3 to 5 minutes. Add the garlic and cook, stirring, for 1 to 2 minutes longer. Turn off the heat and stir in the chives, tarragon, and parsley. Stir in the butter, then season to taste with salt and pepper.

Place the toast on a plate or platter and arrange two pieces of bacon flat on each piece. Add a layer of mustard greens, followed by the mushroom mixture. Crumble the chèvre on top of the mushrooms, drizzle with the remaining olive oil, and serve.

Four 1-inch slices of crusty sourdough or country loaf

2 tablespoons olive oil, plus more for the bread

Kosher salt

Freshly ground black pepper

8 ounces fresh morel mushrooms, cut in half lengthwise

4 slices thick-cut bacon

2 tablespoons malt syrup or molasses

1 shallot, thinly sliced

1 bunch mustard greens, stems trimmed

8 ounces fresh shiitake or cremini mushrooms, cleaned, stemmed, and thinly sliced

2 garlic cloves, thinly sliced

2 tablespoons finely chopped chives

1 tablespoon torn tarragon leaves

¼ cup torn parsley leaves

2 tablespoons unsalted butter

4 ounces chèvre

PAIRING STRATEGY

As if earthy mushrooms and toasted bread weren't enough, the malted bacon plays into the malt of the beer, and the bite of mustard greens and sharpness of chèvre buzz on your tongue with every bubble of carbonation.

RECOMMENDED BEERS

Tim's Brown, Cellarmaker Brewing Company
Nugget Nectar, Tröegs Independent Brewing
Indian Brown Ale, Dogfish Head Craft Brewery

ROASTED GAME HENS WITH MUSHROOM PANZANELLA

When I was cooking in San Francisco, a farmer frequently sold game hens in front of my restaurant. One night I nested them into a preexisting panzanella, and that's where they stayed. The flavor of game hens requires a bold gastrique to balance it out. I like to use a brown ale as the base and sweeten it slightly with some dried currants. While this recipe is great with wild mushrooms and goat cheese, I've tried it with a number of different vegetables and cheeses and it's great every time.

Makes 4 to 6 servings

Preheat the oven to 375°F. Rub the game hens with 2 tablespoons oil and season with salt and pepper. Let rest at room temperature for 15 minutes.

Meanwhile, in a bowl, toss the bread with the remaining olive oil, the thyme, and Parmesan. Season with salt and pepper. Scatter the bread on a rimmed baking sheet and bake until crispy on the outside and golden brown, about 15 minutes. Transfer the croutons to a large bowl and set aside.

Clean the baking sheet and place the hen halves, skin side up, on top. Roast until an instant-read thermometer inserted into the thickest part of the birds reads 155°F, 25 to 35 minutes.

While the game hens are roasting, melt the butter in a skillet over medium-high heat. Add the mushrooms and cook, stirring occasionally, until they start to brown. Add the garlic and the stock; bring the liquid to a simmer and reduce by half. Add the spinach and stir, then season with salt and pepper and remove from heat.

Add the goat cheese to the croutons and toss. Add the mushrooms and any liquid from the pan and toss well.

Make the gastrique: In a small saucepan, bring the sugar and water to a boil and cook until the mixture turns a light amber color, 5 to 7 minutes. Add the brown ale, stirring constantly so the liquid doesn't boil over. Lower the heat to medium-low and reduce the liquid by half. Add the currants and turn off the heat.

Spread the panzanella on a platter and top with the roasted game hens. Spoon some of the gastrique over each game hen and serve.

3 whole game hens, cut in half with the backbones removed

¼ cup plus 2 tablespoons olive oil

Kosher salt

Freshly ground black pepper

3 cups torn sourdough bread (about 1½-inch pieces)

3 thyme sprigs, chopped

¼ cup grated Parmesan cheese

2 tablespoons unsalted butter

2 pounds mixed fresh mushrooms, such as shiitake, cremini, chanterelle, and morel

2 garlic cloves, thinly sliced

1 cup chicken or vegetable stock

2 cups packed spinach leaves

¼ cup fresh goat cheese

½ cup granulated sugar

2 cups water

One 12-ounce bottle brown ale

¼ cup dried currants

PAIRING STRATEGY

Any toasted bread dish works well with Malty & Sweet beers, but this one in particular plays up the earthiness that many of these beers inherently have. The overall depth of these beers tames the gaminess of the meat.

RECOMMENDED BEERS

Fat Tire, New Belgium Brewing Company
Red Rocket Ale, Bear Republic Brewing Co.
Old Brown Dog, Smuttynose Brewing Company

PORK CHOPS WITH MASCARPONE POLENTA, BROWN ALE–GLAZED FIGS, AND COLLARD GREENS

Here, beer is replacing what would usually be a wine or a spirit to glaze the figs, adding the kind of maltiness you'd taste in a good aged ham. While gnawing on those pieces of meat near the rib bone, that extra bit of loin you miss out on with a boneless pork chop, you'll taste why they say, "closer to the bone, the sweeter the meat." The mascarpone adds a level of creaminess to the polenta, making this dish luxurious with accessible ingredients.

Makes 4 servings

Preheat the oven to 350°F. Season the pork chops with salt and pepper and let rest at room temperature for 20 minutes. Place the bacon in a skillet and turn the heat to medium-high. Cook the bacon until golden brown on both sides, about 8 to 10 minutes. Add the onion, sliced garlic, and collard greens and season with salt and pepper. Cook, stirring, for 3 minutes, then add 1 cup of the stock and the water. Bring the liquid to a simmer, cover the pan, and cook for 30 minutes. (Note: If you have time, cook the collards even longer, they can go for up to 2 hours and develop more flavor and tenderness along the way.)

In a medium saucepan, bring 4 cups of stock to a boil. Reduce the heat to low, whisk in the polenta, and continue whisking for 12 to 15 minutes until the polenta is soft and creamy, but not too thick. Season to taste with salt and pepper. Whisk in the mascarpone, cover, and keep warm.

Melt half the butter in a large skillet over high heat. When the foaming subsides, add the pork chops. Cook until browned on one side, 3 to 5 minutes, then turn the chops over and add the remaining butter along with the thyme and smashed garlic. Gently tilt the pan and, using a spoon, baste the butter and herb mixture over the pork chops until the other side is well browned, about 2 minutes. Transfer the skillet to the oven and roast until an instant-read thermometer inserted into the center of the chops reads 145°F, 12 to 15 minutes.

In a saucepan, melt the sugar over medium heat without stirring until it's a light amber color. Carefully add the beer (it'll sputter), bring to a boil, and reduce the liquid until about ¼ cup remains.

Four 10- to 12-ounce bone-in pork chops 2 inches thick

Kosher salt

Freshly ground black pepper

2 strips of thick-cut bacon, diced

1 medium onion, thinly sliced

4 garlic cloves, 2 sliced and 2 smashed

2 bunches collard greens, stems removed, leaves washed and torn into large pieces

6 cups chicken or vegetable stock

1 cup water

2 cups polenta

4 ounces mascarpone cheese

4 tablespoons (½ stick) unsalted butter

3 thyme sprigs

¼ cup granulated sugar

12 ounces brown ale

2 cups fresh figs or ½ cup dried figs, cut into quarters

PAIRING STRATEGY

Here, the Maillard reaction on the pork chops matches the roast of the grain in the brown ale. I amp that up by using brown ale while glazing the figs. This is a case of more is more.

RECOMMENDED BEERS

Runoff Red IPA, Odell Brewing Co.
Boont Amber Ale, Anderson Valley Brewing Company
Ellie's Brown Ale, Avery Brewing Co.

Add the figs and stir until coated in liquid. Add the remaining stock, bring to a boil, and reduce until the sauce is thick enough to coat the back of a spoon.

Divide the polenta among four plates. Top each plate with some of the collard greens and a pork chop. Spoon the brown ale gastrique over the top and serve.

TAGLIATELLE WITH OXTAIL AND TOMATO SUGO

When I walk into someone's house where tomato sauce has been simmering all day, the aroma takes me over with memories of Sunday suppers. Oxtails make a great sugo, a tomato-based sauce with some sort of meat in it generally. Their balance of tender meat to fat give them the ability to add a depth and viscosity to the sauce, and the marrow from the bone melts in like butter. If you can't find oxtails, short ribs are a great substitute. Pasta dough is more forgiving than everyone thinks; it is more of a technique than exact ingredients and quantities, and provides the necessary chew for this mouthwatering sauce.

Makes 4 servings

Make the pasta: In the bowl of a stand mixer fitted with a paddle, combine the 00 and all-purpose flours. Add the eggs and olive oil and mix at medium speed until a shaggy dough forms, about 3 minutes. Mixing the dough in a stand mixer the whole time can result in a harder dough, so I usually turn the dough out onto a work surface and knead with the heel of my hand for at least 3 more minutes, until the dough is smooth and elastic. If you want to keep it in the mixer, do so at a low speed for 3 to 5 minutes. If the dough is still sticky on your fingers, add in a small amount of 00 flour, just enough so your fingers come away clean when you pull them away.

Wrap the dough in plastic and let it sit at room temperature for an hour.

Unwrap the dough and place it on a lightly floured surface. Cut the dough into six pieces. Working with one piece at a time, form the dough into a rough rectangle, then cover with a towel and repeat with the remaining dough. Pass each piece of dough through a pasta machine on the widest setting. Fold the dough in half and pass it through the machine again. Repeat until the dough is the same width as your pasta roller. Continue passing the pasta through the machine, lowering the setting 2 or 3 numbers with each pass and dusting the dough lightly with semolina flour if it sticks, until you've reached the third-thinnest setting. Continue passing the dough through the machine, lowering it one notch at a time until you've reached the second thinnest setting. Dust the pasta lightly with semolina flour and fold it over a few times. Using a knife, cut the pasta

FOR THE PASTA

210 grams tipo 00 flour, plus more for rolling

210 grams all-purpose flour

4 large eggs

1¾ tablespoons olive oil

100 grams semolina flour, for dusting

FOR THE SUGO

4 pounds oxtails (1- to 2-inch lengths)

Kosher salt

Freshly ground black pepper

½ cup olive oil

2 medium carrots, diced

1 large onion, diced

3 to 4 stalks celery, diced

2 garlic cloves, thinly sliced

1 bay leaf

2 thyme sprigs, picked

4 ounces Parmesan cheese rind

One 28-ounce can whole peeled San Marzano tomatoes

1 cup water

Shaved Parmesan cheese, for garnish

½ cup basil leaves, torn, for garnish

PAIRING STRATEGY

Look for a red IPA or rye IPA to add a bit of palate-cleansing spice, or for a warmer, richer mouthfeel, try a barrel-aged strong ale. Dogfish Head Craft Brewery's Sixty-One is a great tomato pairing, blending red wine grapes with a classic IPA. It's a thick dish, full of chew and hearty bites, so having a higher carbonated beer is best, but you don't want anything too hoppy, because that umami is where it's at.

RECOMMENDED BOTTLES

Zoe, Maine Beer Company
Blazing World, Modern Times Beer
Cinder Cone Red Ale, Deschutes Brewery

into long strips about the width of your pinkie. Unfold the pasta and scatter on a baking sheet until ready to cook.

Make the sugo: Rub the oxtails with salt and pepper and let stand at room temperature for 10 minutes.

Heat the oil in a large Dutch oven over medium heat. Add the oxtails and brown on all sides, about 2 to 3 minutes per side. Transfer to a platter and set aside. Add the carrots, onion, and celery to the pot and cook, stirring, until the onion is translucent, around 2 to 3 minutes. Add the garlic, bay leaf, thyme, Parmesan rind, and tomatoes. Stir to break up the tomatoes and add the water. Return the oxtails to the pot, cover and simmer, until the oxtails are very tender, about 2 hours, flipping and checking the meat every 30 minutes or so. Transfer the oxtails to a platter. Pick the meat off the oxtails and discard the bones. Return the meat to the sauce, bring to a simmer, and cook until the sauce has reduced by half. Discard the bay leaf.

Bring a large pot of salted water to a boil and add the pasta. Cook until al dente, 3 to 5 minutes. Strain the pasta and fold immediately into the sauce.

Divide the pasta and sauce among bowls. Top with the shaved Parmesan and basil and serve.

PAN-ROASTED PORK LOIN WITH SQUASH AND SALSA VERDE

Nothing says "Welcome, fall" like the smell of an acorn squash roasting in the oven. A few years back, I served this pork loin and squash dish to my neighbors and spooned some leftover salsa verde over the top, just because I had it. The brightness of the herbs and chile pepped up the whole dish, taking the squash out of its usual one-note place. Ever since, salsa verde has been an expected autumnal condiment and it even has a name: Dimiter Sauce. (Dimiter is my neighbor's name.)

Makes 4 to 6 servings

Preheat the oven to 375°F and line a rimmed baking sheet with foil.

In a bowl, toss the squash with 2 tablespoons of the oil, 3 of the thyme sprigs, and half of the garlic, and season with salt and pepper. Transfer to the prepared baking sheet and set aside.

Season the pork with salt and pepper. Heat the remaining oil in a large, heavy-bottomed skillet over high heat. Place the pork, fatty side down, in the pan and sear until golden brown on all sides. Lower the heat to medium-low and add the butter, the remaining thyme and garlic, and the chile. Using a spoon, slowly baste the hot oil over the pork while cooking, 1 to 2 minutes longer.

Transfer the skillet to the oven and place the squash in the oven as well. Roast until the squash is tender and browned in spots and an instant-read thermometer inserted into the center of the pork reaches 150°F, 30 to 35 minutes. Transfer the pork to a cutting board and let rest for 5 minutes before slicing.

Divide the squash among four plates and arrange the pork slices over the top. Spoon some of the salsa verde around the plate and leave plenty for dipping. Garnish with the pepitas and serve.

1 medium winter squash (3 to 3½ pounds), such as acorn, delicata or butternut, seeded, and cut into 2-inch wedges (only butternut has to be peeled)

¼ cup plus 2 tablespoons canola oil

5 thyme sprigs, picked

6 garlic cloves, smashed

Kosher salt

Freshly ground black pepper

One 2½- to 3-pound boneless pork loin

2 tablespoons unsalted butter

1 Fresno chile, split lengthwise with the seeds, or ¼ teaspoon red pepper flakes

Salsa verde, for serving (recipe follows)

1 cup pumpkin seeds (pepitas), toasted

PAIRING STRATEGY

The caramelization of the pork and squash mimics the sweetness of full-bodied, malty beers. And the hops bring an herbal note into the mix, just like the salsa verde does.

RECOMMENDED BEERS

Amber Ale, Bell's Brewery
Maracaibo Especial, Jolly Pumpkin Artisan Ales
Dunkel Lager, Chuckanut Brewery

SALSA VERDE

Makes 1 cup

In a blender, combine all the ingredients and purée until smooth. Season to taste with salt. The salsa will keep, refrigerated, for up to a week.

2 cups loosely packed parsley leaves

¼ cup loosely packed cilantro leaves

1 Fresno chile, halved and seeded

1 tablespoon sherry vinegar

¼ cup canola oil

1 garlic clove, smashed

Kosher salt

SMOKED BEEF BRISKET WITH ROSEMARY CONFIT POTATOES

Being a native of Kansas City, you have to allow me my burnt ends, those rich and fatty flavorful parts of brisket that hang out in the smoker for just a bit too long, becoming deeply full of flavor. One of my earliest food memories is of ordering burnt ends on bread with pickles, the sauce from the meat seeping into the bread, the pickles giving a piquant crunch. Brisket is a passion for many and an argument for most. It takes a long time to cook and there's no consensus on the right way to do it, but here's my way, which gets to the burnt ends a little bit quicker. There's some added brown ale in the sauce (aka the mop), just to further prove the point that Malty & Sweet beers were made for glazed meats.

Makes 8 to 10 servings

Rub the brisket with salt and pepper (using about ½ teaspoon of each per pound of meat), working it into the meat as well as you can. Place the meat in a dish, cover with plastic wrap, and refrigerate overnight, for at least 12 hours but ideally 24 hours.

Remove the brisket and pat dry with a paper towel.

In a small bowl, combine ⅓ cup ground black pepper, the cayenne pepper, brown sugar, 1 tablespoon of the mustard powder, the onion powder, garlic powder, and ancho chile powder. Mix well and rub all over the brisket. Return the brisket to the dish, cover with plastic and refrigerate for 2 hours, then remove from the refrigerator and let rest at room temperature for 30 minutes.

In a bowl, whisk together the brown ale, tomato paste, and the remaining mustard powder until combined. Set the mop aside.

If you're using a smoker, heat the smoker to 225°F. Place the brisket in the smoker with the fatty side up and smoke until the internal temperature reads 150°F on an instant-read thermometer, 3 to 4 hours. Every hour, rotate the brisket and brush it with the mop.

If you're using an oven, preheat the oven to 250°F. Brush the brisket with mop, then wrap the brisket in heavy-duty foil, making sure it's sealed tight. Place the brisket in a baking pan and roast until it's very tender, about 4 hours. Remove the brisket from the oven and let it rest for 20 minutes before unwrapping it.

10 pounds beef brisket with flap

Kosher salt

Freshly ground black pepper

1 teaspoon cayenne pepper

2 tablespoons brown sugar

2 tablespoons mustard powder

1 tablespoon onion powder

1 tablespoon garlic powder

1 tablespoon ancho chile powder

12 ounces brown ale

2 tablespoons tomato paste

¼ pound (1 stick) unsalted butter

3 rosemary sprigs

2 pounds russet potatoes, skin on, scrubbed, and cut into 2-inch pieces

1 large sweet onion, thinly sliced

PAIRING STRATEGY

Malty & Sweet beers allow this dish's deep, dark, meaty flavors to be celebrated with proper fanfare. The carbonation refreshes with each sip, necessary because, believe you me, you'll want to finish it all.

RECOMMENDED BEERS

Okie, Prairie Artisan Ales
Old Brown Dog, Smuttynose Brewing Company
Face Down Brown, Telluride Brewing Co.

Increase the oven temperature to 375°F and line a rimmed baking sheet with foil. In a saucepan, combine the butter and rosemary and warm over low heat until the butter is melted. In a large bowl, toss the potatoes and onion with the rosemary butter and season with salt and black pepper. Transfer to the prepared baking sheet and roast for 25 minutes or until the potatoes and onions are lightly browned. Remove the baking sheet from the oven and set aside.

Preheat the broiler at low heat. Unwrap the brisket and place it on a rimmed baking sheet fitted with a roasting rack. Broil until a dark, caramelized crust forms on the meat, 5 to 7 minutes. Remove the brisket and let rest for 10 minutes before slicing.

Cut the brisket into ½-inch slices and transfer to a platter. Plate a heaping pile of potatoes and onions on the side and serve.

PORK SHOULDER PASTRAMI

While some might argue that this recipe is a bastardization of pastrami, it's just too damn tasty to fight over. If you live on the east coast, the pastrami making process is taken for granted, as you can walk into any Jewish deli and get a heaping pile of sliced meat, usually enough for two sandwiches with a single order. Anywhere else in the country, you should make your own. Brined and dry rubbed with an aggressive seasoning, this would make any bubbe proud. You'll want to invest in some quality rye bread, which you'll have plenty of time to find during this multiday labor of love.

Makes 8 to 10 servings

Make the brine: In a large stockpot, combine ½ cup salt, ½ cup of the brown sugar, the granulated sugar, pickling spice, smashed garlic, and water. Bring to a boil, then turn off the heat. Let the brine sit for 10 minutes, then add the ice cubes. Let cool to room temperature.

Place the pork in a plastic bag or plastic container and add the brine. Refrigerate for at least 6 hours and up to 24 hours, rotating the pork a few times to ensure even brining.

Remove the pork from the brine and rinse well. Dry with paper towels and set aside.

Combine the black peppercorns, coriander, and mustard seeds in a spice grinder and grind until coarsely ground. Mix the ground spices in a small bowl with the chopped garlic, the remaining brown sugar, and ¼ cup salt. Rub the mixture all over the pork shoulder, working it into the meat with your fingers. Wrap the pork in plastic and refrigerate for 4 hours or up to overnight.

If you're using a smoker, heat the smoker to 225°F. Place the pork in the smoker and smoke until the internal temperature reads 160°F on an instant-read thermometer, about 5 hours. Remove the pork from the smoker and let rest for 20 minutes before slicing.

If you're using an oven, preheat the oven to 375°F and place the pork shoulder on a rimmed baking sheet fitted with a wire rack. Roast until lightly browned, about 35 minutes. Remove the pork and turn the oven down to 225°F. Wrap the pork shoulder tightly in foil, return to the baking sheet, and bake until the internal temperature reads 160°F on an instant-read

Kosher salt

¾ cup light brown sugar

¼ cup granulated sugar

2 tablespoons pickling spice

4 garlic cloves, smashed, plus 4 garlic cloves, finely chopped

5 cups water

3 cups ice cubes

3 pounds boneless pork shoulder

¼ cup black peppercorns

¼ cup coriander seeds

2 tablespoons yellow mustard seeds

8 slices rye bread (1 to 1½ inches thick)

4 slices Gruyère cheese

2 tablespoons canola oil

1 large sweet onion, thinly sliced

PAIRING STRATEGY

The sweetness imparted from the brine, and the spice of the rub, go great with darker wheats, or slightly smoked beers, fortifying the instilled flavors in both the pastrami and beer.

RECOMMENDED BEERS

Dawn of the Red, Ninkasi Brewing Company
Red Wheelbarrow, Maine Beer Company
River Ryed, Sierra Nevada Brewing Co.

thermometer, about for 3 to 4 hours. Remove and let rest for 20 minutes before removing from foil.

Increase the oven temperature to 450°F. Top the rye bread slices with the Gruyère and arrange on a baking sheet. Toast until the cheese is melted and beginning to brown. Remove and set aside.

In a small skillet, heat the oil over medium heat. Add the onion and sauté until lightly browned, 7 to 9 minutes. For

extra flavor, add any drippings left from the pork. Remove from the heat and set aside.

Thinly slice the pork. Top the bread with a layer of onions, followed by a layer of pork, and serve.

BUTTERSCOTCH BUDINO WITH BROWN ALE CARAMEL

The first dessert I ever had at Town Hall, a restaurant I frequented late night in San Francisco, was a butterscotch and chocolate pot de crème. There's not a week that goes by that I don't think of those flavors. This is my tribute to that treat, a creamy butterscotch budino (Italian for pudding) with a thick brown ale caramel and dark chocolate toffee; a new spin on a favorite end-of-night reward.

Makes 6 to 8 servings

Heat a high-sided saucepan over medium heat. Add the brown sugar, water, and ¼ teaspoon of the salt. Cook until mixture becomes very dark, about 10 minutes. Very quickly add the cream and milk, whisking immediately to keep it from boiling over. Whisk until the mixture heats back up and becomes smooth. Lower the heat to medium low, add the beer, and gently simmer until the liquid is thick enough to coat the back of a spoon, 15 to 20 minutes.

In a medium bowl, whisk together the egg, egg yolks, and cornstarch. Slowly add 1 cup of the caramel cream mixture to the egg mixture. Whisk until smooth, then begin adding this mixture back to the pan. Once combined, bring the liquid to a boil and remove from the heat. Add 2 tablespoons of the butter. Strain the mixture through a fine-mesh sieve and divide among and ramekins or glasses. Cover the puddings with plastic and chill until set, at least 3 and up to 24 hours.

Line a rimmed baking sheet with foil and brush it with oil. In a large saucepan, combine the granulated sugar, the remaining butter, and the remaining salt. Cook over medium-high heat until an inserted instant-read thermometer reads 285°F, brushing any crystals that form on the side of the pan with water. As soon as the mixture reaches 285°F, pour it into the prepared baking sheet. Spread the chocolate chips over the caramel and allow them to melt. Spread the melted chocolate evenly over the top and sprinkle with the chopped hazelnuts. Let the toffee cool to room temperature, about 45 minutes.

Break the toffee into pieces. Scatter the toffee pieces over each serving of budino and serve with the whipped cream.

¾ cup dark brown sugar

⅓ cup water

½ teaspoon kosher salt

1¾ cups heavy cream

¾ cup whole milk

1 tablespoon dark beer, such as a brown ale or stout

1 large egg

2 egg yolks

2 tablespoons cornstarch

3 tablespoons unsalted butter

1 tablespoon canola oil

1 cup granulated sugar

1 cup dark chocolate chips

½ cup chopped hazelnuts

Lightly sweetened softly whipped cream, for serving

PAIRING STRATEGY

This dessert also speaks to the classic nature of Malty & Sweet beers—they've survived the test of time for a reason: they're balanced, they give the full spectrum of flavor that a well-rounded meal would, they hit all the marks when it comes to what one wants in comfort food, and they're terrific with the crispy and browned flavors of this dessert.

RECOMMENDED BEERS

Palo Santo Marron, Dogfish Head Craft Brewery
Bigfoot, Sierra Nevada Brewing Co.
Solstice D'hiver, Brasserie Dieu du Ciel

GINGERBREAD AND MOLASSES COOKIES

I didn't grow up enjoying gingerbread—I actually despised those ornate candy houses people built during Christmas, the old spices were often rancid and the added frosting was too sickly sweet. I do have a soft spot for these cookies though, and have even asked pastry chefs I've worked with to issue me a daily ration. What makes these great is that they're chewy in the middle and also have crispy edges, so you get the spectrum of texture—something for everybody.

Makes about 20 cookies

Preheat the oven to 350°F and line two rimmed baking sheets with parchment.

In a stand mixer fitted with the paddle attachment, cream the butter and 1 cup of the sugar on medium speed until light and fluffy, about 4 minutes. Add the molasses, baking soda, salt, cinnamon, and all three forms of ginger; mix until well combined. Add the eggs and beat at medium speed for 1 minute, stopping halfway through to scrape the sides and bottom of the bowl. Add the flour and beat at low speed until just combined. Using a spatula, scrape the sides of the bowl and mix into the dough.

Pour the remaining sugar into a bowl. Take about 2 tablespoons of dough and roll it into a ball. Roll the ball in the sugar and place on a baking sheet, then press down lightly to flatten the ball into a disk. Repeat with the remaining dough, leaving 3 inches between cookies.

Bake the cookies until lightly brown around the edges, about 12 minutes, and let cool on the baking sheets for 5 minutes before transferring to a wire rack to cool completely.

1 cup (2 sticks) unsalted butter

1½ cups granulated sugar

½ cup molasses

2 teaspoons baking soda

1 teaspoon kosher salt

1 teaspoon ground cinnamon

½ teaspoon ground ginger

1 tablespoon finely chopped candied ginger

1 teaspoon finely grated fresh ginger

2 large eggs

3½ cups all-purpose flour

PAIRING STRATEGY

Cinnamon and other warming spices are flattering companions for Malty & Sweet beers. The body of the beers is full enough to stand up to three forms of ginger (ground, candied, and fresh).

RECOMMENDED BEERS

Toaster Pastry, 21st Amendment Brewery
Tocobaga Red Ale, Cigar City Brewing
Shallow Grave, Heretic Brewing Company

GARRETT MARRERO

MAUI BREWING CO.

Garrett Marrero of Hawaii's Maui Brewing Co. left a well-paying job in San Francisco to open a brewery in the middle of an ocean. An island at the vanguard of permaculture, Maui, as a place and brewery, looked toward how the beer market pandered to the drinking public, "women drink light and fruity beers, men drink big beers and IPAs." A concerted effort was made to blend in mainland culture and not to succumb to mainstream drinking norms. Hawaii nurutred people drinking what they liked, but also what tasted great with their native cuisine, like grilled huli-huli chicken, barbecued over mesquite wood basted with a sweet, sticky sauce. It had smoke, fruit, spice, tanginess, and a bite. From there, Pineapple Mana Wheat, an American pale wheat ale, was born. Not for that recipe specifically, but reflecting the culture and flavors of where Marrero brewed. Marrero is originally from San Diego, but didn't see a west coast style IPA as the way to go with the indigenous cuisine, tying the local agriculture to both the dish and the glass in front of a guest: Bikini Blonder Lager with smoked fish, Coconut Hiwa Porter (the first commercial coconut beer) with bananas foster (while most people would initially gravitate to chocolate), and of course a nice pilsner with fresh ahi poke.

ON DRAFT

COCONUT HIWA PORTER
One of the first darker beers that moved outside of dessert land. It complements duck, lamb, and beef and has the ability to be one of the most flexible dark beers out there, full of hand-toasted coconut, not extract. If you go to the brewery on a day they're toasting it, it's quite a treat.

PINEAPPLE MANA WHEAT
Ideal with sorbet and sherbet, this is one of the most refreshing beers out there. Again, a ton of fresh ingredients: Maui Gold pineapple, plus tropical Tettnanger and Liberty hops.

CHAPTER 04

RICH & ROASTY

These beers bring intensely deep, dark flavors: barrel-aged bourbon, vanilla, chocolate, and in some cases, a burnt or smoky aroma. The range of dishes that works with these beers includes those that have roasted fats like the ones present in nuts, as well as the iron content and minerality found in red meats. You might already know the pleasure of the darkest chocolate you can find with a stout; use that mode of thought and think about dessert: cake and cookies already rely on richness, so why not bring some more into the fold?

These craft beers are focused on dark roasted malts; with aromas from coffee to cocoa, they linger on the finish. The more intense the style, the more pronounced the deep, stewed flavors of dates, figs, cherries, and plums. In pairing, use ingredients that can hold up to these stronger styles of beer, which include brown ales, oatmeal stouts, black wheat schwarzbier, and robust porters. Even though these beers taste like deeply roasted grains, dark chocolate, and espresso, they're often lighter on the palate than you'd assume, so you can go heavier with the food, like roasted nuts, braised meats, and chocolate desserts.

With notes of chocolate and coffee, these beers can be described as deep, dark, creamy, and rich. They work well with deep flavors of foods that are charred and grilled. On the simple side, anything with a clean briny finish (like oysters) will work as well, they will replace the salt on the palate with roasted flavors. Go on the richer side, and see how this style intensifies your palate; roast a fatty cut of red meat and a stout will pull out the richness in the meat's marbling. Braise something and taste how the beer rounds out the palate.

SOME RICH & ROASTY
BEER STYLES

Brown Ale

Imperial Stout

Irish Dry Stout

Milk Stout

Oatmeal Stout

Porter

Schwarzbier

108
GRILLED RIB-EYES WITH HEIRLOOM TOMATOES AND LITTLE GEM SALAD

111
BRAISED LAMB SHANKS

112
HANGER STEAK WITH TATER TOTS AND BEER MUSTARD

114
BEEF SHORT RIBS WITH CELERY ROOT PURÉE AND PLUM-BRAISED FENNEL

116
CHOCOLATE DEVIL'S FOOD CAKE WITH MINI STOUT MILKSHAKES

119
COFFEE AND COCOA POTS DE CRÈME

120
POPPY SEED POUND CAKE WITH MILK CHOCOLATE MOUSSE AND CANDIED PECANS

122
PEANUT BUTTER SEMIFREDDO WITH CANDIED PEANUTS AND DARK CHOCOLATE CARAMEL

125
MALTED OAT PECAN COOKIES

126
DARK CHOCOLATE SOUFFLÉS WITH BOURBON BARREL CRÈME ANGLAISE

RICH & ROASTY
FOOD FRIENDS

Brown butter, chocolate (milk and dark), coffee, eggplant, lamb, lentils, oysters, parsnips, peanuts, pecans, raisins, salt, smoke, star anise, toffee, whiskey, vanilla

GRILLED RIB-EYES WITH HEIRLOOM TOMATOES AND LITTLE GEM SALAD

This, my friends, is a worthy dish to splurge on. Get a well-marbled rib-eye, the ripest tomatoes, and super soft blue cheese and let the artistry of each ingredient speak for itself. I know it sounds a little like an entrée and two sides, but it's really a "meat and three" when you consider the deeply roasted grains in the beer.

Makes 4 servings

Put the tomatoes in a bowl, season with salt and pepper, and toss with the olive oil. Let sit at room temperature to marinate.

Prepare a medium-hot charcoal or gas grill. Season the steaks with salt and pepper. Grill the steaks until well browned on one side, about 5 minutes, then flip and continue cooking to your desired doneness, about 5 minutes for medium rare. Transfer the steaks to a cutting board and let rest.

In a small bowl, whisk together the red wine vinegar, canola oil, and 2 tablespoons of the tomato marinating liquid. Add the lettuce, toss well, and season with salt and pepper.

Arrange the tomatoes and lettuce on a platter. Slice the steaks into ½-inch pieces and arrange on top of the lettuce and tomatoes. Top the steaks with the blue cheese crumbles and the herbs. Drizzle more tomato marinating liquid over the dish and serve.

4 large heirloom tomatoes cut into 1- to 2-inch pieces

Kosher salt

Freshly ground black pepper

2 tablespoons olive oil

Two 12- to 14-ounce beef rib-eye steaks

1 tablespoon red wine vinegar

2 tablespoons canola oil

4 heads Little Gem lettuce or 1 head butter or other leaf lettuce, separated into leaves and washed

½ cup crumbled blue cheese

2 tablespoons finely chopped chives

2 tablespoons dill fronds

¼ cup parsley leaves

PAIRING STRATEGY

Usually you see a side of starch (e.g. fried or mashed potatoes) with such a hearty cut of meat, but in this case, the beer acts as part of the trio, standing up to the beefiness of this cut, the acidity of the tomatoes, and the saltiness of the cheese, rounding out this dish into a complete meal.

RECOMMENDED BEERS

The Butcher, Societe Brewing Company
Virginia Black Bear, Lickinghole Creek Craft Brewery
Shotgun Wedding, Country Boy Brewing

BRAISED LAMB SHANKS

A few winters spent cooking in the skiing mecca of Vail, Colorado, brought out my desire to serve large cuts of meat in the dishes they'd been cooked in. There's something so great about removing the lid of an enormous Dutch oven tableside, allowing the aromas to greet your guests, especially when fresh snow is falling just outside the windows. Here, lamb shanks are seared, the pan deglazed with dark beer, and the meat left to braise, covered, for a few hours, until it becomes tender in its own juices. To tone down the gaminess of the lamb, I like to infuse the cooking liquid with fennel seeds and star anise, which add a spicy depth to this hearty dish.

Makes 4 to 6 servings

Rub the lamb shanks with the tomato paste, salt, pepper, fennel seeds, and star anise. Cover and refrigerate for 4 hours, up to overnight.

Preheat the oven to 350°F.

Heat the oil in a heavy-bottomed saucepan or Dutch oven over high heat. Sear the lamb shanks on all sides until golden brown. Remove the lamb shanks from the pan and set aside. Add the onion, carrot, and celery to the pan and cook over medium heat until the onion is translucent, 2 to 3 minutes. Add the flour and cook for 1 minute. Deglaze the pan with the beer, scraping up any browned bits on the bottom of the pot with a wooden spoon. Simmer the liquid until reduced by about one third. Add the stock, thyme, garlic, and bay leaf. Cover the pot and transfer it to the oven. Braise until the lamb is very tender, 2½ to 3 hours. Transfer the lamb shanks to a platter and cover with foil. Strain the braising liquid into a saucepan. Bring the liquid to a simmer and reduce until it's thick enough to coat the back of a spoon.

Serve in the Dutch oven or transfer the lamb shanks to a platter. Spoon the sauce over the lamb shanks and serve.

4 lamb shanks, about 1 pound each

3 tablespoons tomato paste

Kosher salt

Freshly ground black pepper

1 teaspoon fennel seeds

2 star anise

2 tablespoons canola oil

1 large sweet onion, roughly chopped

2 medium carrots, peeled and roughly chopped

1 celery stalk, chopped

1 tablespoon all-purpose flour

12 ounces dark beer (such as brown ale, porter, or stout)

4 cups vegetable or chicken stock

3 thyme sprigs

2 garlic cloves, smashed

1 bay leaf

PAIRING STRATEGY

Beers with dried fruit and smoky aromas are strong enough to stand up to lamb's gaminess, and create a smoothness on the palate. They complement anything made with dark spices, like star anise, cloves, or nutmeg.

RECOMMENDED BEERS

Allagash Black, Allagash Brewing Company
Dry Irish Stout, Brooklyn Brewery
Smoked Porter, Alaskan Brewing Co.

HANGER STEAK WITH TATER TOTS AND BEER MUSTARD

A hanger steak with an easy shallot sauce makes a great weeknight meal—even better when served with tater tots. I've become a little obsessed with tots. I like mine to be part creamy potato, part shredded potato, almost as if a tater tot met a croquette at a bar. They're all the better to mop up steak juices this way. They can be made ahead and frozen, too. Just make sure to keep a pot of beer mustard handy.

Makes 6 servings

Place the cut up potatoes with garlic cloves in a large saucepan and cover them with cold water. Season with salt and boil the potatoes until tender, 20 to 25 minutes. Strain the potatoes and garlic, reserving ¼ cup of the cooking water, and purée in a blender until smooth.

Place the remaining whole potatoes in the saucepan and cover with cold water; season with salt. Bring the water to a boil, lower the heat, and simmer for 5 minutes. Drain the potatoes and let them cool to room temperature. Shred the potatoes on a box grater into a mixing bowl. Add 2 tablespoons of the flour and the chives. Add the potato purée and mix well with a wooden spoon. Season to taste with salt and pepper.

Scoop 1 tablespoon of the potato mixture and form it into a ball, pressing out any air, then roll it into a cylinder. Place the tater tot on a baking sheet and repeat with the remaining potato mixture. Refrigerate the tater tots for 30 minutes to set.

In a shallow bowl, whisk together the eggs and milk. Place the remaining flour in another bowl. Remove the tater tots from the refrigerator and, working with one at a time, dip a tater tot into the egg mixture, shaking off any excess, then roll the tot in the flour. Place on the baking sheet and repeat with the remaining tots. Refrigerate the tots for 30 minutes.

Preheat the oven to 250°F. Heat a medium skillet over medium-high heat and add ¼ cup of canola oil, making sure to cover the bottom of the pan with ¼ inch of oil. Once the oil is hot, fry the tater tots in batches, stirring frequently, until golden brown on all sides. Using a slotted spoon, transfer the tots to a baking sheet. Repeat until all the tots are done frying and transfer the tray to the oven for 5 minutes.

2 pounds russet potatoes, peeled, and cut into 2-inch pieces, plus 1 pound russet potatoes, peeled and left whole

3 garlic cloves, thinly sliced

Kosher salt

Freshly ground black pepper

1 cup plus 2 tablespoons all-purpose flour

1 tablespoon finely chopped chives

2 large eggs

1 tablespoon whole milk

¼ cup plus 2 tablespoons canola oil

2 pounds hanger steak, trimmed

2 tablespoons unsalted butter

6 medium shallots, finely chopped

1 bay leaf

1 teaspoon granulated sugar

1 cup chicken stock

¼ cup chopped parsley leaves

Beer mustard, for serving (see page 187)

PAIRING STRATEGY

The deep satisfaction of a hanger steak is only made better by a Rich & Roasty beer whose malts exalt the shallot pan sauce to a place of decadence.

RECOMMENDED BEERS

Kalamazoo Stout, Bell's Brewery
Old No. 38 Stout, North Coast Brewing Co.
Back in Black, 21st Amendment Brewery

Season the hanger steak with salt and pepper. In a skillet, heat the remaining canola over high heat. Add the hanger steak and cook until the bottom is well browned, about 5 minutes. Turn the steak over and add the butter. Continue cooking until the internal temperature of the steak reaches 140°F on an instant-read thermometer, about 5 minutes longer for medium rare. Transfer the steak to a plate and let rest.

Heat the skillet used to cook the steak over medium heat. Add the shallots, bay leaf, and sugar to cook, stirring, until the shallots are lightly browned, 3 to 5 minutes. Add the chicken stock, bring the liquid to a simmer and reduce until the sauce is thick enough to coat the back of a spoon. Turn off the heat, discard the bay leaf, stir in the parsley, and set aside.

Slice the hanger steak against the grain and plate on a platter or divide evenly among six plates. Arrange the tots around the steak and spoon the shallot sauce on top of the steak. Serve with the mustard on the side.

BEEF SHORT RIBS WITH CELERY ROOT PURÉE AND PLUM-BRAISED FENNEL

Short ribs are one of the most flavorful cuts of beef out there, yet they're often overlooked because of their toughness and length of time to cook. Believe me, the reward is definitely worth it! I hate to say it, but short ribs are sexy, they come out so lush and warm and it's really a meal to woo your mate. To showcase the meat, I opted for a lighter celery root purée, as opposed to the commonly used mashed potato; it allows the beef to be the star of the plate.

Makes 6 servings

Preheat the oven to 350°F. Season the short ribs with salt and pepper and let rest at room temperature for 5 minutes.

In a heavy-bottomed saucepan or Dutch oven, heat 3 tablespoons of the oil over high heat. Sear the short ribs on each side until dark brown, working in batches if necessary (don't crowd the pan). Add the tomato paste and lower the heat to medium. Add the onions, carrots, and celery and cook, stirring, until lightly browned, 3 to 5 minutes. Add the garlic and flour, stirring to coat the vegetables, and cook for 3 minutes. Deglaze the pan with the beer, scraping up any browned bits on the bottom of the pot with a wooden spoon. Simmer the liquid until reduced by about one third. Add the stock, thyme, oregano, and bay leaf. Bring to a boil, cover the pot, and place in the oven. Braise until the meat is tender, 2½ to 3 hours. (Note: Boneless ribs or smaller ribs will cook more quickly.)

Carefully remove the ribs from the liquid and transfer to a plate. Strain the braising liquid into a saucepan, then add the short ribs to that pot. Set the pot over low heat to keep the ribs warm.

In a medium saucepan, combine the celery root and enough cold salted water to cover. Bring the liquid to a boil and cook until the celery root is tender, about 30 minutes. Drain the celery root and transfer to a food processor or blender along with the heavy cream and butter. Process until smooth and season to taste with salt. Keep warm.

Heat the remaining oil in a skillet over high heat. Add the fennel and sear on both sides until golden brown. Lower the heat to medium, add the plums, and cook for 2 minutes.

5 pounds bone-in beef short ribs, or 3½ pounds boneless short ribs

Kosher salt

Freshly ground black pepper

¼ cup plus 1 tablespoon canola oil

2 tablespoons tomato paste

1 large sweet onion, roughly chopped

2 medium carrots, peeled and roughly chopped

2 celery stalks, roughly chopped

4 garlic cloves, thinly sliced

1 tablespoon all-purpose flour

12 ounces dark beer (such as brown ale, porter, or stout)

6 cups chicken, vegetable, or beef stock

4 thyme sprigs

1 tablespoon dried oregano

1 bay leaf

2 pounds celery root, peeled and cut into 2-inch pieces

½ cup heavy cream

2 tablespoons unsalted butter

2 fennel bulbs, cored and cut into wedges, fronds reserved for garnish

6 plums, halved and pitted

PAIRING STRATEGY

To balance the creamy celery root with some tartness, I rely on the subtle sour notes from the plums, which are in contrast to the more cooked fruit flavors you can find in Rich & Roasty beer.

RECOMMENDED BEERS

Stout, Sierra Nevada Brewing Co.
Coconut Hiwa Porter, Maui Brewing Co.
Big Cone Black Ale, Figueroa Mountain Brewing Co.

Take 1 cup of liquid from the short ribs and add it to the fennel and plums. Bring to a simmer and reduce until the sauce is thick enough to coat the back of a spoon.

Divide the celery root purée among six plates. Distribute the short ribs and fennel among the plates. Spoon some of the plum sauce over the short ribs, garnish with fennel fronds, and serve.

CHOCOLATE DEVIL'S FOOD CAKE WITH MINI STOUT MILKSHAKES

Why not double down on dessert—that's what the devil would do, right? Adding a milkshake to the party, with syncopated sips of stout to bites of dark chocolate, will bring you back to the malt shop era, that time your parents speak about when pharmacies served tulip glasses of a frothy shake with a slice of freshly baked cake. It was considered a cure-all, an elixir of life even, or at least a way to take the edge off.

Makes 8 servings

Make the ganache: In a small saucepan, bring the cream to a boil. Place the chocolate in a heatproof bowl and slowly pour the cream over the chocolate, stirring until the chocolate has melted. Add the butter and stir until smooth. Set aside.

Make the cake: Preheat the oven to 350°F and grease two 8-inch round cake pans with butter, then flour them. Shake out any excess flour and set aside.

Using a stand mixer fitted with the paddle attachment, cream the butter, brown sugar, and vanilla at medium speed until very light and fluffy, about 5 minutes. Add the eggs and mix until blended. Add the baking soda and powder and mix until combined. In a separate bowl, sift the flour and cocoa powder together. Add half of the flour mixture to the egg and butter mixture and mix at low speed, stopping to scrape the sides and bottom of the bowl as needed. Add the remaining flour mixture along with the buttermilk and salt and mix until smooth. Using a spatula, add ¼ cup of the ganache and mix until blended, making sure to scrape the sides and bottom of the bowl.

Divide the batter between the cake pans. Bake until the edges of the cake begin to pull away from the sides of the pans, 35 to 40 minutes. Remove the cakes from the oven and let cool for 6 minutes in the pan before turning out onto a wire rack to cool completely.

Slice each cake in half horizontally. Put the first layer on a serving plate and spread it evenly with ¼ of the remaining ganache. Set the second layer on top and spread with another layer of ganache. Continue layering until you have a four-tier cake with three layers of ganache in between. If the ganache is too firm, warm it over a double boiler until it softens. Once

FOR THE GANACHE

3 cups heavy cream

1½ pounds 60% or 70% dark chocolate, chopped

2 tablespoons unsalted butter, room temperature

FOR THE CAKE

1 cup (2 sticks) unsalted butter at room temperature, plus more for greasing the pans

1¾ cups all-purpose flour, plus more for the pan

2 cups brown sugar

1 vanilla bean, seeds scraped, or 1 teaspoon vanilla bean paste

3 large eggs

1 teaspoon baking soda

1 teaspoon baking powder

¾ cup Dutch process cocoa powder

1½ cups buttermilk

1 teaspoon kosher salt

FOR THE MILKSHAKES

2 pints good-quality vanilla bean or chocolate ice cream

12 ounces bottled milk stout beer

PAIRING STRATEGY

The only thing better than chocolate is more chocolate. Here, matching malts to elementary flavors makes big sense.

RECOMMENDED BEERS

Milk Stout Nitro, Left Hand Brewing Company
Obsidian Stout, Deschutes Brewery
Great Commander, Lickinghole Creek Craft Brewery

the cake is whole, pour the remaining ganache over the cake and use a small offset spatula to spread it around the sides if needed. Let the ganache rest while you make the shakes.

Put the ice cream in a blender. Turn the machine on to low speed and slowly add the stout, blending until you get a creamy consistency. Pour the shakes into glasses and serve with the cake.

COFFEE AND COCOA POTS DE CRÈME

Pots de crème *have graced my dessert menus throughout my entire culinary career. These little luxurious puddings are incredibly satisfying, while also being relatively easy to make, and they'll keep for a couple days in the refrigerator. Chocolate is a classic pot de crème flavor, but I like to add a little espresso to mine to give them a deeper, slightly bitter note that's a nice end to a meal.*

Makes 6 to 8 servings

Preheat the oven to 300°F.

In a small saucepan, bring the cream, milk, espresso powder, and salt to a simmer. Place the chocolate in a heatproof bowl, pour the cream mixture over the chocolate, and whisk until smooth.

In a separate bowl, whisk the egg yolks with the sugar until smooth. Slowly add the chocolate mixture to the egg yolk mixture and whisk until blended. Strain the mixture into a clean bowl and divide among small ramekins. Transfer the ramekins to a baking pan and add enough hot water to reach three-quarters up the sides of the ramekins. Transfer the pan to the oven and bake until the *pots de crème* are set around the edges but slightly loose in the center, 20 to 30 minutes (baking time will depend on the size of the ramekins).

Transfer the *pots de crème* to the refrigerator and chill for at least 2 hours or overnight.

To serve, top the *pots de crème* with the whipped cream and chocolate shavings.

1¾ cups heavy cream

½ cup whole milk

1 teaspoon instant espresso powder

¼ teaspoon kosher salt

8 ounces dark chocolate, chopped

6 large egg yolks

2 tablespoons plus 1 teaspoon sugar

Lightly sweetened whipped cream and shaved dark chocolate, for serving

PAIRING STRATEGY

While rich, smooth *pots de crème* are texturally light, like the head of a great stout, the dark coffee flavor in these accentuates the roasted malt quality of the beer.

RECOMMENDED BEERS

Yeti, Great Divide Brewing Company
Black Chocolate Stout, Brooklyn Brewery
Kalamazoo Stout, Bell's Brewery

POPPY SEED POUND CAKE WITH MILK CHOCOLATE MOUSSE AND CANDIED PECANS

I think every chef should be able to make a pound cake; it's a great go-to when you need a quick, yet tasty dessert. The pound to pound ratio makes it as user friendly as possible for those of us who shy away from exact measurements while baking. The versatility of the recipe means that you can change the cake itself dramatically by simply adding berries, nuts, or chocolate to the batter. Or just plate a slab of cake and use it as a base for toppings like whipped cream and fruit or whatever you have on hand. Poppy seeds in pound cake isn't exactly unexpected, but I like turning what could be seen as a breakfast cake into an end-of-meal treat with the addition of fluffy milk chocolate mousse and candied pecans.

Makes 8 to 10 servings

Preheat the oven to 350°F. Use 2 tablespoons of the butter to grease a 1 pound (8-by-4-inch) loaf pan. Add ¼ cup flour and coat the inside of the pan. Shake out any excess flour.

In a bowl, cream the remaining butter and 1 cup of the sugar until well blended. Add the buttermilk and eggs and whisk until combined. Add the baking powder, baking soda, salt, and the poppy seeds and mix until well combined. Add the remaining flour and mix until just combined. Pour the batter into prepared pan and bake until a toothpick comes out clean from the center of the loaf, about 45 minutes.

In a bowl, whisk together 1 tablespoon plus 2 teaspoons water and the confectioners' sugar until smooth. Brush the icing over the top of the pound cake as soon as it comes out of the oven. Wait about 10 minutes before turning the cake out onto a wire rack. Turn the oven down to 250°F.

Bring about 4 cups of water to a simmer in a medium saucepan. Place the chocolate in a heatproof bowl that will fit over the top of the saucepan. Once the water is simmering, place the bowl over the water and stir until the chocolate is melted and smooth. Set aside and let cool to room temperature. In a separate bowl or the bowl of a stand mixer fitted with the whisk attachment, beat the heavy cream until stiff peaks form. Fold

1 cup (2 sticks) unsalted butter, at room temperature

2 cups all-purpose flour

1½ cups granulated sugar

½ cup buttermilk

3 large eggs

1½ teaspoons baking powder

½ teaspoon baking soda

1 teaspoon kosher salt

2 tablespoons poppy seeds

3 tablespoons plus 2 teaspoons water

¼ cup confectioners' sugar

14 ounces milk chocolate (not more than 60% cacao), chopped

2 cups heavy cream

1 egg white

8 ounces pecan pieces or halves

PAIRING STRATEGY

Even though Rich & Roasty beers look sort of hefty because of their color, they tend to end with a light finish, thanks to carbonation. The same is true of this dessert, the lush mousse and the toasted pecans providing nice textural contrasts to the dense cake.

RECOMMENDED BEERS

Mean Old Tom, Maine Beer Company
Edmund Fitzgerald Porter, Great Lakes Brewing Co.
Schwarzbier, Duck-Rabbit Craft Brewery

the melted chocolate into the whipped cream and mix until blended. Chill for 20 minutes.

Line a rimmed baking sheet with foil. In a medium bowl, whisk the egg white and the remaining water until frothy. Add the pecans and toss to coat. Add the remaining sugar and the salt and stir until the pecans are evenly coated. Scatter the pecans on the prepared baking sheet and bake, stirring occasionally, until browned, about 45 minutes. Remove from the oven and let cool.

To serve, slice the pound cake and divide among plates. Top each slice with a generous dollop of chocolate mousse and sprinkle with the candied pecans.

PEANUT BUTTER SEMIFREDDO WITH CANDIED PEANUTS AND DARK CHOCOLATE CARAMEL

I'm an absolute sucker for peanut butter and chocolate in any combination, and this semifreddo is just a grown-up version of that affinity. Semifreddo ("half cold," in Italian) is just that, somewhere texturally between ice cream and a whipped mousse. To get both of my favorite flavors into each bite, I freeze a lightly sweet peanut butter base and then pile slices of the peanut butter semifreddo with homemade candied peanuts and my signature dark chocolate caramel sauce. Stop reading this and make it now.

Makes 4 to 6 servings

Make the semifreddo: In a medium saucepan, bring the water to boil. Place a medium bowl in the freezer.

In another bowl that will fit over the pot, combine the egg yolks, vanilla paste or seeds, ½ cup of the sugar, and salt. Once the water comes to a boil, place the bowl with the yolk and sugar mixture over the water and whisk constantly until smooth ribbons appear, about 5 to 7 minutes. Remove from the heat and quickly scrape the mixture out into the bowl from the freezer. Stir until cool.

Line a 1-pound loaf pan with plastic wrap. In a stand mixer fitted with the whisk attachment, combine the heavy cream and the remaining sugar. Whisk until stiff peaks form, then transfer to another bowl; set aside. Put the peanut butter and cooled egg mixture in the bowl of the stand mixer and beat until smooth. Using a rubber spatula, fold in one-third of the whipped cream and mix until well blended. Gently fold in the remaining whipped cream. Using a spatula, transfer the mixture to the prepared loaf pan and cover tightly with plastic. Press down gently to remove excess air bubbles and freeze for at least 4 hours before serving.

Make the candied peanuts: Preheat the oven to 300°F and line a rimmed baking sheet with foil.

In a medium saucepan over medium heat, combine the sugar and water. Once the sugar dissolves in the water, add the peanuts. Stir until the water has evaporated and the sugar is coating the peanuts, about 10 to 12 minutes. Scatter the

FOR THE SEMIFREDDO

4 cups water

4 egg yolks

1 teaspoon vanilla bean paste (or scrapings of 1 vanilla pod)

¾ cup granulated sugar

¼ teaspoon kosher salt

1½ cups heavy cream

¾ cup smooth peanut butter

FOR THE CANDIED PEANUTS

¾ cup granulated sugar

¼ cup water

1½ cups roasted skinless peanuts

FOR THE DARK CHOCOLATE CARAMEL

¾ cup heavy cream

⅓ cup granulated sugar

¾ cup water

½ cup dark chocolate, finely chopped

PAIRING STRATEGY

This dessert pairs nicely with any chocolate-inflected stout, but since the dessert is so sweet on its own, I almost prefer it with a not-sweet black wheat schwarzbier with a pronounced dark chocolate–like bitterness.

RECOMMENDED BEERS

Breakfast Stout, Founders Brewing Co.
Dark Star, Fremont Brewing
Russian Imperial Stout, Stone Brewing

peanuts on the prepared baking sheet and bake, stirring occasionally, until nicely browned and fragrant, about for 30 minutes. Remove from the oven and set aside.

Make the dark chocolate caramel: Place the heavy cream in a medium bowl and set aside.

In a medium saucepan, combine the sugar and water. Bring to a simmer over medium-high heat and cook until the sugar turns golden brown, 5 to 7 minutes. Remove from the heat and

pour into the bowl with the heavy cream. The mixture will bubble and the sugar will set a bit. Transfer the mixture back to the saucepan and place over medium heat. Allow the sugar to fully dissolve in the cream. Add the chopped chocolate and stir until dissolved. Keep warm.

Cut the semifreddo into 1- to 2-inch slices. Transfer each slice to a bowl or plate, drizzle with some of the caramel sauce, sprinkle with candied peanuts, and serve.

MALTED OAT PECAN COOKIES

I might have hated granola bars as a kid, but I love oat cookies now, an affection that might have grown out of a love for beer. Cooking with beer ingredients is a natural way to create recipes that will go well with the beer. For these cookies, I use malted barley flour, which is made in the same way that barley is malted for making beer. Barley grains are germinated, to convert starches to sugar, by adding water. This process is stopped by drying the grains. At this point, the barley either heads to a brewery or to a mill where it's ground up into a slightly sweet flour. These cookies find added complexity with the addition of malted barley flour, and I hope they will be a gateway for you to substitute malted grains for regular ones in other recipes. If your sweet tooth is calling, add 1 cup of chocolate chips to the final dough.

Makes about 24 cookies

Preheat the oven to 350°F and line a baking sheet with parchment or a silicone baking mat.

Using a stand mixer fitted with the paddle attachment, beat the butter and both sugars together at medium-high speed until light and fluffy. Add the vanilla, cinnamon, salt, and baking soda and mix until well combined. Add the eggs and mix until smooth and creamy.

In a separate bowl, whisk the two flours together. Add half of the flour mixture to the egg mixture and mix until just combined. Add the remaining flour mixture and mix, scraping the sides and bottom of the bowl. Stir in the pecans and oats (and chocolate chips, if using) with a rubber spatula until well combined.

Form the dough into 1- or 2-tablespoon balls. Place the cookies 2 inches apart on the baking sheet. Bake until the cookies are golden brown, 10 to 13 minutes, then transfer the cookies to a wire rack and let cool completely before serving.

½ cup (1 stick) unsalted butter, at room temperature

1 cup brown sugar

¾ cup granulated sugar

1 teaspoon pure vanilla extract

½ teaspoon ground cinnamon

1 teaspoon kosher salt

1 teaspoon baking soda

2 large eggs

½ cup malted barley flour

1 cup all-purpose flour

2 cups chopped pecans

1 cup rolled oats

1 cup chocolate chips (optional)

PAIRING STRATEGY

Even if you leave chocolate out of these cookies, the aroma of cocoa in the beer might be enough. I bet a nice glass of chocolatey porter will replace the milk you used to dunk your cookies in.

RECOMMENDED BEERS

Indian Brown, Dogfish Head Craft Brewery
Komodo Dragonfly, Upland Brewing Co.
Cutthroat Porter, Odell Brewing Co.

DARK CHOCOLATE SOUFFLÉS WITH BOURBON BARREL CRÈME ANGLAISE

My first job out of culinary school was working at the American Restaurant in Kansas City under chefs Michael Smith and Debbie Gold. I started in the pantry station, putting together cold appetizers and salads, with the added random task of making soufflés to order. Soufflés have a reputation for being finicky and time consuming, but having served thousands of these suckers, I know that when done right, they can be downright amazing. The secret is patience, and a deft hand; this will take some practice, but certainly not a thousand times over, I've already done that for you, so this should be a cinch.

Makes 6 servings

Make the crème anglaise: In a saucepan, bring the cream and vanilla seeds (or paste) to a simmer and turn off the heat.

In a medium bowl, whisk together the egg yolks, sugar, and the beer until smooth. Add ¼ cup of the cream mixture and stir to incorporate. Pour the cream and egg mixture back into the saucepan and stir to combine. Heat the mixture over low heat until the sauce is thick enough to coat the back of a spoon, about 5 minutes. Remove from the heat and strain into a bowl. Cover the crème anglaise with plastic and refrigerate for at least 1 hour and up to overnight.

Make the soufflés: Preheat the oven to 350°F and brush the bottom and sides of six 4-inch ramekins with butter. Add ¼ cup of the sugar to the buttered ramekins and rotate to evenly coat the inside. Shake out any excess sugar.

In a medium saucepan, bring the water to a simmer. In a medium heatproof bowl, combine the butter and chocolate. Place the bowl over the water and heat, stirring frequently, until the chocolate is completely melted and evenly blended. Remove the bowl and set aside.

In a stand mixer fitted with the whisk attachment, beat the egg whites and salt at medium-high speed until soft peaks form. Add the remaining sugar and beat until stiff peaks form.

In a separate bowl, whisk the egg yolks until smooth. Add the egg yolks to the chocolate mixture and stir until incorporated. Using a rubber spatula, fold the egg whites gently into the chocolate mixture. Divide the batter among the ramekins, filling each about three-quarters full.

FOR THE CRÈME ANGLAISE

½ cup heavy cream

1 vanilla bean, split and seeds scraped (or 1 teaspoon vanilla bean paste)

3 large egg yolks

2 tablespoons granulated sugar

1 tablespoon bourbon barrel–aged beer

FOR THE SOUFFLÉS

¼ cup unsalted butter (½ stick), plus softened butter for greasing the ramekins

½ cup granulated sugar

4 cups water

5 ounces dark chocolate, finely chopped

4 egg whites

⅛ teaspoon kosher salt

3 large egg yolks

PAIRING STRATEGY

The soufflés' light texture combined with the rich bourbon crème anglaise only gets richer, and more decadent by the intensity of a deep, dark, and roasty beer.

RECOMMENDED BEERS

Mean Old Tom, Maine Beer Company
Bell's Cherry Stout, Bell's Brewery
Ten Fidy, Oskar Blues Brewery
Goodnight Bodacious, Short's Brewing Company

Place the soufflés on a baking sheet and transfer to the oven. Bake in the middle of the oven until the soufflés have puffed but are slightly jiggly in the center, about 20 minutes.

To serve, make a small hole in the center of each soufflé and pour some of the crème anglaise into the hole. Serve immediately.

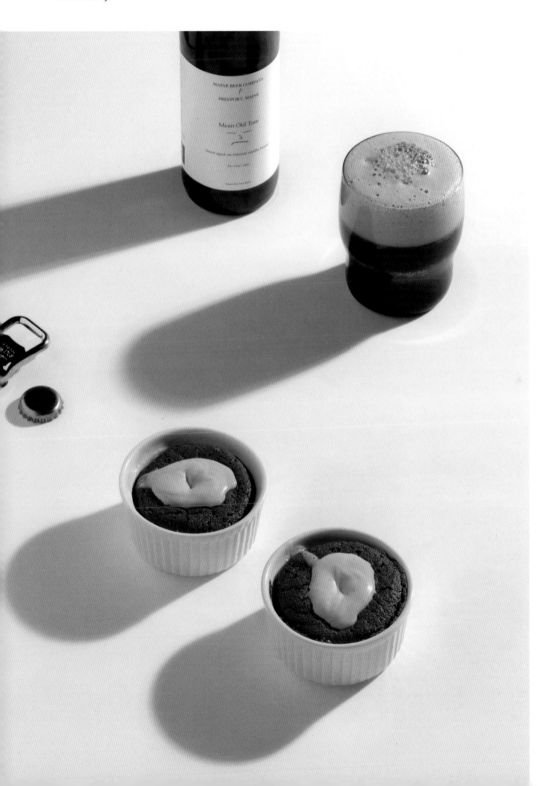

STEVEN PAUWELS

BOULEVARD BREWING COMPANY

S teven Pauwels of Boulevard Brewing Company in Kansas City, Missouri, has seen the growth of craft breweries on every corner since his start in 1989. Pauwels believes the biggest change to have happened is in the kitchen; where menus were once limited to pizzas and fried foods, brewpubs have become verifiable restaurants; even in tasting rooms, you'll find great snacks with your samples. But he's wary of how drinkers understand the interplay between beer and food. Pauwels used to brew a Chocolate Ale with Christopher Elbow, a local chocolatier. The beer was a huge success and everyone wanted to pair it with a chocolate dessert, but that overwhelmed the chocolate flavor in the beer. Tomatoes are amazing in the Midwest, but that doesn't mean tomatoes and just any beer are a good idea. That's why he made Tank 7, a farmhouse ale that is meant to pair with everything!

ON DRAFT

TANK 7 FARMHOUSE ALE
The canon of what a saison can be, this beer unlocked what beer and food pairings could do for me. I've served this beer with seared scallops, asparagus, strawberries, salmon, and duck. This beer was first described to me in wine terms (e.g. crisp, minerality, peppery, floral, aromatic, like a Sauvignon Blanc, Chablis, Sancerre).

UNFILTERED WHEAT BEER
Steven uses yeast to bottle-condition this beer, which contributes to its flavor and texture. Citrusy, bready, and slightly sweet, it's pretty light-bodied even though it's cloudy. It pairs best with a hot summer day, running the range from oysters on the half shell to roasted chicken and stone fruits.

CHAPTER 05

FRUITY & SPICY

More than anything else, we're making the yeast work in this section. Flavors in these beers are mainly driven by the yeast, sometimes by the barrel; with notes of stone fruits, citrus, ginger, a bit of caper-like salt. Yeast produces flavor characteristics found in other food and beverage products, but we're not used to tasting its effect other than in wine and bread. You'll get banana, clove, barnyard hay, but the power is not only on the palate, it's also in the aroma, which catches some drinkers off guard. These recipes highlight different strains of yeast, and how their flavors contribute to making a specific beer taste as such. Here you'll find recipe ingredients that have also been used in the beer-making process, lending themselves to the overall flavor of the pairing, which will leave you wondering where the flavor actually came from, the food or the beer?

While still showcasing malt and hops, these craft beers are more about dominant fruit and spices. The spice flavors come from the yeast, and to enhance the fruity notes, actual fruit purée or whole fruit may be added to the brewing process. Some of these beers are brighter and have tart stone fruit and citrus flavors, like Belgian wits such as hefeweizen and saison. Some are warmer, spiced with clove, pepper, and vanilla, like hop-less gruits, trappist strong ales, tripels, and quadrupels. With such spicy aromatics, richer foods that would go well with rosés or deep red wines would work well here. These beers are exactly what they sound like, full of fruit and spice, and are best with the ingredients already associated with those beers. More cooked than fresh fruits, like compotes and candied fruit, these beers also go well with foods that are spiced with ginger or coriander, as well as warming spices.

SOME FRUITY & SPICY BEER STYLES

Belgian Blond Ale

Belgian Wit

Gruit

Hefeweizen

Quadrupel

Saison

Tripel

FRUITY & SPICY
FOOD FRIENDS

Buttermilk, candied ginger, farro, game meat, grapefruit, grapes, horseradish, mussels, olive oil, orange, oregano, peach, pear, rutabaga, vinegar

CARROT, ORANGE, AND GINGER SOUP

After some time spent working in kitchens in France, you learn that when you strive to make the most perfect tournée, brunoise, or julienne, most of your early knife skills end up taking shape as carrot soup. While carrots do make up the backbone of so many things, from stocks to sauces, braises and roasts, they can also stand alone quite poignantly. In this perfectly velvety soup, the creaminess of the carrot is highlighted with a kick of ginger and orange's acid and oil, making something scrumptious out of what would otherwise be scraps.

Makes 6 servings

Heat the oil in a large saucepan or Dutch oven over medium heat. Add the carrots and cook, stirring frequently, until lightly browned, about 2 to 3 minutes. Add the onion and cook, stirring until translucent, about 2 to 3 minutes. Add the butter, ginger, garlic, and orange zest, and cook until aromatic, about 2 minutes. Add the stock and bring the mixture to a simmer. Cover and cook until the vegetables are tender, 30 to 35 minutes.

Transfer the soup to a food processor or blender and purée until smooth. Strain the soup into a clean saucepan and keep warm over low heat. Stir in the heavy cream. Season to taste with salt and pepper.

In a bowl, whisk the orange juice into the crème fraîche. Divide the soup among six bowls and top each with a spoonful of crème fraîche. Garnish with the chives and serve.

¼ cup olive oil

4 cups chopped carrots (about 6 to 8 large carrots)

1 medium sweet onion, chopped

¼ cup (½ stick) unsalted butter

3 tablespoons finely grated fresh ginger

2 garlic cloves, thinly sliced

Finely grated zest and juice of 1 medium orange

4 cups vegetable stock

¼ cup heavy cream

Kosher salt

Freshly ground black pepper

6 tablespoons crème fraîche

2 tablespoons finely chopped chives

PAIRING STRATEGY

Carrot goes so well with fruit and spice that you'll find a gamut of tart-to-warm expressions in these beers. Try this with a saison and a gruit (a beer using herbs or botanicals in place of hops) just for comparison's sake.

RECOMMENDED BEERS

Alaskan White, Alaskan Brewing Co.
Orange Ave. Wit, Coronado Brewing Co.
Autumn Maple, The Bruery

SEARED SCALLOPS WITH PARSNIPS, CAPERS, AND RAISINS

My philosophy about scallops is the antithesis of Coquilles St.-Jacques, that rich and creamy gratinéed scallop dish that the French have been making for centuries. I'm not into entirely masking the flavor of the mollusks. To me, scallops should be seared well, and then served simply with salty and sweet things to accent their freshness. This recipe is mostly about assembly. I roast wedges of parsnips to intensify their sweetness and warm up a little topping of capers and golden raisins, all of which meet nicely seared scallops on a plate.

Makes 4 to 6 servings

In a small bowl, cover the raisins with the hot water. Wait 1 minute, then stir in the vinegar. Set aside.

Preheat the oven to 350°F and line a rimmed baking sheet with foil.

In a bowl, combine the parsnips, lemon slices, and 1 tablespoon of the oil. Toss until everything is coated in oil, then season with salt and pepper. Transfer the parsnips and lemon to the prepared baking sheet. Roast until the parsnips are tender and golden brown, 15 to 20 minutes. Remove from the oven and set aside.

In a skillet, heat the remaining oil over high heat until it shimmers. Season the scallops with salt and place in the skillet. Cook without moving the scallops until browned on the bottom, 3 to 5 minutes. Add half of the butter to the pan and turn the scallops over. Continue cooking the scallops while basting with the butter until just cooked through, 2 to 3 minutes longer. Transfer the scallops to a plate and let rest.

Wipe out the skillet and add the remaining butter. Heat the butter over medium heat until it begins to brown, then add the capers, raisins (in their liquid), and chives. Cook, stirring, for 1 minute, then remove from the heat.

Divide the parsnips among plates and add 2 or 3 scallops to each plate. Spoon the sauce over the scallops and serve.

1/4 cup golden raisins

1 tablespoon hot water

1 tablespoon champagne vinegar

1 pound parsnips, peeled and cut into wedges

1 lemon, thinly sliced

2 tablespoons canola oil

Kosher salt

Freshly ground black pepper

8 to 12 scallops (U 12-20), abductor muscles removed

2 tablespoons unsalted butter

2 tablespoons capers, drained

1 tablespoon finely chopped chives

PAIRING STRATEGY

Shellfish pairs so well with wits and saisons. In this dish, the beer highlights the sweetness of the scallops and the parsnips and echoes the fruitiness of the raisins.

RECOMMENDED BEERS

Golden Monkey, Victory Brewing Company
Company Colette, Great Divide Brewing
Saison Au Miel, Left Hand Brewing Company

BELGIAN BEER–STEAMED MUSSELS

The Belgians do it right with moules frites. At its most basic level, that dish is composed of mussels steamed in an aromatic broth (often made with beer) and served with a mess of crispy fries. Tons upon tons have seen this treatment, with cooks around the world putting their own spin on the crucially important steaming liquid. My version, which starts with a Belgian wit, uses Fresno chiles, basil, and is finished with butter, giving a little bit of heat, herbal notes, and richness to the dish, leaving plenty of broth for the requisite day-old baguettes to soak up.

Makes 4 to 6 servings

In a large saucepan, heat the oil over medium-high heat. Add the mussels and stir to coat. Add the garlic, shallot, and chile and cook for 1 minute. Add the beer, bring to a simmer, and reduce by one third. Add the vegetable stock and season with salt and pepper. Cover the pot, leaving a crack for steam to escape, and steam until the mussels open, 5 to 6 minutes (discard any mussels that don't open). Add the butter and stir to combine. Add the thyme, parsley, and basil and toss.

Serve immediately with crusty bread for dipping.

1 tablespoon canola oil

2 pounds mussels, cleaned and debearded

2 garlic cloves, thinly sliced

1 small shallot, finely chopped

1 Fresno chile, thinly sliced (seeds removed if desired)

½ cup Belgian wit beer

½ cup vegetable stock

Kosher salt

Freshly ground black pepper

2 tablespoons unsalted butter

1 teaspoon chopped thyme

1 tablespoon chopped parsley

¼ cup thinly sliced basil

Crusty baguette, for serving

PAIRING STRATEGY

A Belgian wit is a natural with this. The soft carbonation of the beer opens up the aromatics of the dish and lends bright, citrusy notes for a clean finish.

RECOMMENDED BEERS

Allagash White, Allagash Brewing Company
Witte, Brewery Ommegang
Namaste White, Dogfish Head Craft Brewery

LEMON CORIANDER CHICKEN WITH PAN-FRIED POTATOES AND SPICED YOGURT

The best meals I had on a trip through Spain over a decade ago were served family style. I'll often break down a few chickens and roast them when hosting a big group. It's easy for everyone to just take what they want. Here, I rub chicken with a lemony herb blend first and then cook until golden brown, served alongside crispy potatoes to soak up the juices, with a peppery, spiced yogurt dip.

Makes 4 to 6 servings

In a large bowl, combine the canola oil with the garlic, thyme, coriander, and half of the paprika. Add the chicken pieces and season with salt and pepper. Using your hands, work the spice mixture evenly into the chicken pieces. Cover and refrigerate for at least 2 hours or up to overnight.

In a bowl, combine the yogurt, the juice and zest of 1 lemon, the caraway, the remaining paprika, and the cumin. Season to taste with salt.

Preheat the oven to 375°F and line a rimmed baking sheet with foil. Place the chicken pieces, skin side up, on the sheet and roast until the skin is golden brown and the meat is cooked through, 30 to 35 minutes.

While the chicken is roasting, place a medium skillet over medium-high heat and add 1 inch of canola oil heating until an inserted instant-read thermometer reads 350°F. Working in batches if necessary (don't crowd the pan), add the potatoes and fry, stirring frequently, until tender and golden brown on all sides, about 2 to 3 minutes. Using a slotted spoon, transfer the potatoes to a paper towel–lined plate to drain. Season with salt and keep warm in a pan on the back of the stove, then flash for 3 minutes in the oven before serving.

Remove the chicken from the oven and squeeze the remaining lemon juice over the chicken. Transfer the chicken and any juices to a bowl and add the chopped cilantro. Toss well.

Arrange the potatoes and chicken on a platter and garnish with the torn cilantro leaves. Serve with the spiced yogurt on the side.

¼ cup canola oil, plus more for frying

6 garlic cloves, thinly sliced

4 thyme sprigs, chopped

2 teaspoons ground coriander

1½ tablespoons paprika

1 whole chicken, separated into breasts, legs and thighs, breasts cut in half

Kosher salt

Freshly ground black pepper

1 cup plain Greek yogurt

4 lemons, juiced, plus finely grated zest of 1 lemon

½ teaspoon ground caraway

½ teaspoon ground cumin

3 pounds russet potatoes, peeled and cut into 1-inch cubes

1 bunch cilantro, half coarsely chopped, half in torn leaves

PAIRING STRATEGY

Lemon and coriander flavors are no strangers to saison-style beers, which makes them a no-brainer for this every-man-for-himself feast.

RECOMMENDED BEERS

Saison de Lis, Perennial Artisan Ales
Hoppy Table Beer, Allagash Brewing Company
Four Play, Upright Brewing

WHITE SEA BASS WITH ASPARAGUS AND PRESERVED LEMON

A few years ago, I organized a bunch of chefs to help cook a beer dinner at the James Beard House in New York. I'd planned to make sea bass en papillote, cooking the fish with asparagus and herbs in a little paper pouch. When half of the chefs were forced to bail after a snowstorm canceled hundreds of flights, the idea of folding over 100 little envelopes was abandoned too. Instead, I infused all of the flavor for the sea bass and asparagus into this buttery Mediterranean shallot sauce, using preserved lemons, tarragon, and olives to give an aromatic burst at the table, without the crafty presentation.

Makes 4 servings

Preheat the oven to 350°F and line a rimmed baking sheet with foil.

Bring a pot of salted water to a boil and blanch the asparagus for 2 to 3 minutes. Remove and run under cold water or place in an ice bath to stop the cooking. Set aside.

In a medium skillet, heat the oil over high heat. Season the sea bass with salt and place the fish, skin side down, in the skillet. Cook until the skin is crisp and golden brown, 5 to 7 minutes. Transfer the fish, skin side up, to the baking sheet. Roast the fish until cooked through, 7 to 10 minutes.

Meanwhile, drain the oil from the pan and wipe clean. Return the pan to medium heat and add half of the butter and all of the shallots. Cook, stirring frequently, until the shallots are soft, 3 to 5 minutes. Add the preserved lemon juice and rind and stir well. Turn the heat to low, stir in the remaining butter, and cook until the butter is melted, 1 to 2 minutes. Add the tarragon and olives, remove from the heat, and set aside.

In a medium skillet, bring ¼ cup of water to a simmer. Add the asparagus and cook until warmed through (add more water if needed to cover them completely), then drain and season with salt.

Arrange the asparagus and fish, skin side up, on a platter. Spoon the sauce over and serve.

1 bunch (about 18 spears) asparagus, trimmed

2 tablespoons canola oil

Four 5-ounce sea bass fillets, with skin

Kosher salt

¼ cup (½ stick) unsalted butter

2 medium shallots, thinly sliced

2 tablespoons preserved lemon juice (see page 185)

1 tablespoon preserved lemon rind, finely chopped (see page 185)

2 tablespoons torn tarragon leaves

8 Castelvetrano or similar green olives, quartered

PAIRING STRATEGY

Asparagus is a notoriously difficult vegetable to pair drinks with, but beer works handily. Fruity & Spicy beers play nicely with the preserved lemons, while the sea bass acts as a conduit for the beer, providing texture, while the beer fills in as seasoning.

RECOMMENDED BEERS

Tank 7 Farmhouse Ale, Boulevard Brewing Company
Oak Aged Bretta, Logsdon Farmhouse Ales
Hennepin, Brewery Ommegang

GRAIN-STUFFED QUAIL WITH ROASTED ROOT VEGETABLES AND HUCKLEBERRY VINAIGRETTE

I love the gentle gamey notes of quail in the fall, especially with roasted root vegetables. I usually look for whole quails sold "semi-boneless," with the center breastbone and spine removed because they are more easily stuffed. Lately, I've been using grains like farro and quinoa as the base for stuffing smaller poultry, as it just holds up better and gives a nice nuttiness to this autumnal dish. To brighten up the overall toastiness of the dish, I make a tart huckleberry vinaigrette with sherry vinegar. Blackberries or raspberries are fine alternatives to huckleberries, but they're a bit sweeter, which means you'll add a little extra vinegar to up the acid.

Makes 4 servings

In a large skillet, heat 1 tablespoon of the oil over medium high heat. Add the diced carrot and onion and season with salt and pepper. Cook until the onion is translucent, about 2 to 3 minutes. Stir in the stock and a third of the garlic. Add 2 tablespoons of the butter and the chopped parsley and stir until incorporated.

Combine the cooked grains in a bowl and add the carrot–onion mixture and stir to combine. Using a spoon, stuff each quail with the grain mixture.

Preheat the oven to 375°F and line a rimmed baking sheet with foil.

In a bowl, toss the root vegetables and onion quarters with the thyme, the remaining garlic, and the chile and season with salt and pepper. Scatter the vegetables on the baking sheet and roast until tender and golden brown, about 15 minutes. Remove from the oven and set aside.

Season the quail with salt and pepper. In a large skillet, heat the remaining oil over high heat. Add the quail, breast side down, and cook until browned, 2 to 3 minutes. Carefully turn the quail over and add the remaining butter. Continue cooking, using a spoon to baste the quail with the oil and butter mixture, until browned on the other side, about 5 minutes longer. If the pan gets too hot, turn the heat down to medium high. Transfer the quail to the prepared baking sheet. Roast until an instant-read thermometer inserted into the thickest part of the meat reads

¼ cup canola oil

1 carrot, peeled and cut into ⅛-inch dice

1 large sweet onion, half cut into ⅛-inch dice, half quartered

Kosher salt

Freshly ground black pepper

¼ cup chicken or vegetable stock

3 garlic cloves, thinly sliced

¼ cup (½ stick) unsalted butter

2 tablespoons finely chopped parsley

¾ cup cooked quinoa

¾ cup cooked farro

2 pounds mixed root vegetables, such as carrots, celery root, parsnips, peeled and cut into 1- to 2-inch pieces

4 quail, semi-boneless (back and breastbones removed), rinsed and patted dry

3 thyme sprigs, chopped

1 Fresno chile, halved lengthwise and seeded

2 tablespoons sherry vinegar

½ cup fresh huckleberries

2 tablespoons olive oil

155°F, 25 to 30 minutes. Transfer the quail to a platter and cover with foil to keep warm.

Empty the skillet used to cook the quail (but don't wipe the pan clean). Heat the pan over medium heat and add the vinegar, scraping up any browned bits with a wooden spoon. Add the huckleberries and the olive oil. Bring the liquid to a simmer, then turn off the heat.

Divide the roasted vegetables among four plates and place the quail on top. Spoon the vinaigrette over the quail and serve.

COQ AU SAISON

Coq au vin is a traditional French dish of chicken, bacon lardons, and mushrooms, typically braised in a deep red Burgundy. All across France, there are many variations of this recipe depending on the wine of the region. In Alsace, aromatic white wine is used, in the south, it might be rosé. For our unique craft beer approach, this recipe has been adapted to bring out the peppery spice of a saison, just as in France. This recipe can be made richer by swapping the saison out for a dubbel, which doesn't spike the alcohol too high, but keeps a good amount of spice in the braise. Served over mashed potatoes, this dish is a perfect pairing for a cool spring evening or a cold autumn night.

Makes 4 servings

Brine the chicken for 4 to 6 hours.

Remove the chicken from the brine and pat dry with paper towels. In a large, heavy-bottomed saucepan or Dutch oven, heat the oil over medium heat. Add the bacon and cook until lightly browned and crisp, 3 to 5 minutes. Using a slotted spoon, transfer the bacon to a paper towel–lined plate and set aside, leaving the bacon fat in the pan.

Heat the pan with the bacon fat over medium-high heat. Season the chicken pieces with salt and pepper and place them, skin side down, in the pan. Cook until browned on all sides, 7 to 11 minutes. Transfer the chicken to a platter. Add the thyme, bay leaf, garlic, and onions to the pan and cook, stirring, for 1 minute. Add the mushrooms and deglaze the pan with the beer, scraping up any browned bits with a wooden spoon. Season with salt and pepper. Return the chicken to the pot and add the stock. Bring the liquid to a simmer, cover the pot, and cook for 30 minutes. Uncover the pot and continue simmering until the chicken is cooked through and sauce has thickened, about 25 minutes longer. Add the butter and stir to coat the chicken and mushrooms. Discard the bay leaf.

Sprinkle the reserved bacon over the chicken and vegetables and serve.

1 whole chicken, broken into 2 breasts, 2 thighs, and 2 legs

1 recipe Beer Brine for Pork and Poultry using a saison (see page 189)

2 tablespoons olive oil

2 slices thick-cut bacon, cut crosswise into ¼-inch lardons

Kosher salt

Freshly ground black pepper

2 thyme sprigs

1 bay leaf

3 garlic cloves, thinly sliced

12 cipollini onions, peeled

1 pound fresh crimini, shiitake, or chanterelle mushrooms

¼ cup saison (or brown ale/dubbel for a richer version)

2 cups chicken stock

2 tablespoons unsalted butter

PAIRING STRATEGY

Pair this, of course, with a saison. Look for the carbonation to release the fat from your tongue and for the spice to complement the warmth of the dish. If you're looking for something just a little bit richer, feel free to pair this with a brown ale or a dubbel.

RECOMMENDED BEERS

Interlude, Allagash Brewing Company
Saison Rue, The Bruery
Tank 7 Farmhouse Ale, Boulevard Brewing Company

OLIVE OIL CAKE

Olive oil and honey work well with bitter, sour, and sweet flavors, so this cake has a broad pairing spectrum. It's deceivingly tasty for how simple it is. It's really a blank slate for other flavors as well, a seasoned setting for experimentation. I like using grassier and greener olive oils, which can stand up to stronger beers.

Makes 8 servings

Preheat the oven to 350°F and grease a 9-inch round cake pan with baking spray.

In a stand mixer fitted with the whisk attachment, beat the eggs and sugar at medium speed until they've doubled in volume. Add the oil, honey, lemon zest and juice, and salt and mix until well combined. In another bowl, whisk together the flour, cornmeal, and baking powder until just combined. With the mixer on low speed, add the flour mix into the egg and sugar mix, and beat slowly until just combined. Use a spatula to scrape down the sides and bottom of the bowl.

Pour the batter into the prepared pan and bake for 12 minutes. Rotate the cake and bake until a toothpick inserted into the center comes out clean, another 12 to 15 minutes longer.

While the cake bakes, in a small bowl, whisk together the water and confectioner's sugar until smooth. Brush the top of the cake with the icing as soon as it comes out of the oven. Let the cake cool in the pan for 5 minutes before turning it out onto a wire rack to cool for at least 15 minutes before slicing and serving.

4 large eggs

1 cup granulated sugar

¾ cup olive oil

2 tablespoons honey

Finely grated zest and juice of 2 lemons

1 teaspoon kosher salt

1½ cups all-purpose flour

¾ cup cornmeal

2 teaspoons baking powder

2 tablespoons water

½ cup confectioners' sugar

PAIRING STRATEGY

Try tripels and quads with this and see how they'll bring out the spiciness of the olive oil as well.

RECOMMENDED BEERS

Surette, Crooked Stave Artisan Beer Project
Saison Bernice, Sante Adairius Rustic Ales
Freaky Peach, Tröegs Independent Brewing
All I See Is Carrion, Adroit Theory

MALTED QUINOA RICE PUDDING

This dessert was created specifically for Maui Brewing Co.'s hazy, hoppy, and intensely juicy Pineapple Mana Wheat beer. In an attempt to avoid the all too frequently rich and heavy beer and dessert pairing situation, I cooked malted quinoa rice pudding–style and went determinedly down the tropical route, decking the pudding out with guava syrup, lime, and toasted coconut flakes.

Makes 8 servings

In a saucepan, combine the quinoa, milk, 2 cups of the heavy cream, $1/3$ cup of the sugar, salt, and the vanilla. Cook over medium-low heat, stirring and scraping the bottom of the pot frequently with a rubber spatula, until the quinoa is tender, about 15 minutes. Transfer to a bowl, cover with plastic, and refrigerate until needed.

In a small saucepan, combine the guava purée with 3 tablespoons of the sugar and bring to a boil. Transfer to a heatproof container and refrigerate.

In a small bowl, whisk the remaining heavy cream with the remaining sugar until stiff peaks form. Whisk in the lime juice and zest and set aside.

Spoon the quinoa pudding into bowls and top with the whipped cream. Drizzle with the guava syrup. Garnish each bowl with 1 or 2 lime suprêmes and a sprinkle of toasted coconut.

$1\frac{1}{2}$ cups malted quinoa (available at health food stores or online), rinsed with warm water and drained

1 cup whole milk

$2\frac{1}{2}$ cups heavy cream

$1/3$ cup plus 5 tablespoons granulated sugar

$1/4$ teaspoon kosher salt

$1/2$ teaspoon vanilla bean paste (or scrapings of $1/2$ vanilla pod)

$1/4$ cup guava purée, found in freezer aisles

Finely grated zest and juice of 4 limes, plus suprêmes of 2 limes (see the technique on page 32)

$1/4$ cup toasted unsweetened coconut flakes

PAIRING STRATEGY

With the popularity of fruit-forward beers these days, it's increasingly easy to find a hefeweizen with a juicy tropical flavor profile. The muskiness of the guava and zestiness of the lime in this dish draw great east and hop parallels.

RECOMMENDED BEERS

Seizoen Bretta, Logsdon Farmhouse Ales
Pineapple Mana Wheat, Maui Brewing Co.
Otra Vez, Sierra Nevada Brewing Co.

DOUGLAS CONSTANTINER & TRAVIS SMITH

SOCIETE BREWING COMPANY

S ociete Brewing Company in San Diego, California, was founded in 2012. Douglas Constantiner and Travis Smith, formally of The Bruery and Russian River Brewing Company, saw very few fine-dining establishments giving beer a proper spotlight on their menus, so they decided to do something about it. Maybe beer seemed too blue-collar or pedestrian, but they saw their customers treating beer as an ultimate affordable luxury. You can purchase a beer for $5 to $8, which is a pretty low investment compared to shelling out $80 for a bottle of wine. You can arguably try 10 different beers for that price! It will get you outside the comfort zone of imperial stouts with chocolate cake, hefeweizens with weisswurst sausage. Those pairings are givens, and we're looking to expand the mind of what's possible. At one particular dinner at Societe, I made a *bistecca fiorentina* (an Italian T-bone steak) with olive oil on the side; diners were instructed to pour the olive oil on the steak, then take a sip of the Societe's The Pupil, an IPA. The beer has such huge aroma, stone fruit and citrus, like a fruity Tuscan olive oil. Even Douglas was quizzical before he had a bite, exclaiming that the beer is notoriously tough to pair. Now, as a tasting note, this food pairing comes before the beer description. We served a vegetable panzanella with The Gleaner, a saison, and a pork and shelling bean cassoulet with The Debutante, a Belgian amber ale. This helped prove my point, that matching intensity and strength should be a general guiding principle for food-beer pairings. Pairing "by the book" gives you a basis, but that way you forget to smell the beer and really taste it on the palate.

ON DRAFT

THE PUPIL/THE APPRENTICE
Two fresh, young, exciting takes on west coast pale and IPA, with touches like a big dose of hops, and big malt on the palate too.

THE URCHIN
Part of a barrel-aged series; a feral ale with Grenache blanc grapes from San Diego County's Vesper Vineyards. It can stand up to funk, and has plenty of its own.

CHAPTER 06

SOUR, TART, & FUNKY

I hate to say it, but bugs and bacteria are what we're working with here. Whether it's making super-dry beers through the use of brettanomyces yeast, or jaw-puckering ones through lacto-fermentation/pediococcus, most of these beers are commonly barrel-aged. There is often an addition fruit and/or other ingredients that have natural sugars in them to accentuate the flavors and tartness. Tart is like biting into an apple, it quickly pops then goes away, whereas sour stays with you. Funky is confusing because most people think that means sour and tart, but it's more like wild and damp; they're acquired tastes. If you like things like gorgonzola cheese, you'll like these. There's an earthy profile across the board, a nice amount of malt and yeast, and they also show a strong connection between the flavors in the beer and the ingredients in the food.

Sour beers have lately become the darlings of the craft beer industry. Farmhouse, leather, hay, grass, and even wet socks aren't necessarily what you want to think of when choosing a beverage, but if you like acidic biodynamic wines, you'll love this family of beer. They're gentle, lighter malts with a ABV, and have a body perfect for making them your new session ale of choice. Berliner weisse and gose leave your palate almost bone dry, with a spritz of citrus. Pair with delicate foods, like raw or barely cooked seafood, allowing the raw ingredients to shine. Fresh fruits like strawberries, tart cherries, rhubarb, and pomegranate are often added to lambics and gueze. Berries and stone fruit are great additions to paired dishes, as they only reinforce the beer's inherent flavor and benefit from its sweetness. Flanders ales are a little more vinegary, but make a great sweet and sour sauce when reduced.

These beers are acidic, bright, minerally, jammy, vinous, barrel-aged, woody, and can stand up to funk because of their lacto-fermentation. Think aged meats, assertive fruit flavors, and strong dairy.

SOME SOUR, TART, & FUNKY BEER STYLES

American Brett

American Sour

Flanders Ale

Gose

Gueze

Lambic

SOUR, TART, & FUNKY
FOOD FRIENDS

Apricots, balsamic, basil, bay leaf, cherries, chutney, gorgonzola, goat cheese, juniper, liver, melons, pineapple, pomegranate, prosciutto, roe, sourdough, winter squash, yogurt

CHICKEN LIVER AND QUADRUPEL ALE MOUSSE

A classic French chicken liver mousse is ordinarily made with cognac, but I like to swap out the brandy for a quadrupel ale, giving the mousse an earthy richness that complements the underlying flavor of the chicken liver itself. Here, beer truly enhances the recipe as an ingredient, but also pairs brilliantly with the dish as well.

Makes 6 to 8 servings

In a bowl, cover the chicken livers with the milk. Cover and refrigerate overnight. Drain and discard the milk. Rinse the livers and dry with a paper towel.

In a medium skillet, melt 2 tablespoons of the butter over medium-high heat. Season the chicken livers with 1½ teaspoons salt and ½ teaspoons pepper and add to the pan. Cook until one side is lightly brown, about 4 minutes. Turn the livers over and add the shallots. Cook until the shallots are translucent and the chicken livers are cooked through, 5 to 7 minutes. Add the beer, bring to a simmer, and cook for 1 minute.

Transfer the contents of the pan to a food processor and let cool for 5 minutes. Turn the food processor on and, with the machine running, slowly add the remaining butter. Blend until smooth.

Place a fine mesh strainer over a bowl. Using a rubber spatula, push the mousse through the strainer. Rinse the spatula and discard the contents left in the strainer.

Use the spatula to pack the mousse into ramekins or jars. Cover and refrigerate for at least 2 hours or overnight.

Serve the mousse with the crackers or toasted baguette, and topped with capers, parsley, and red onion.

1 pound chicken livers, cleaned

2 cups whole milk

¾ cup (1½ sticks) unsalted butter, at room temperature

Kosher salt

Freshly ground black pepper

1 shallot, finely chopped

¼ cup quadrupel ale

Crackers or toasted baguette slices

2 tablespoons capers, drained

¾ cup loosely packed parsley leaves

¼ cup finely chopped red onion

PAIRING STRATEGY

Look to pair this dish with a rich quadrupel, or if you want, you can try a stronger sour or tart beer to break up the dark liver flavor, putting focus on the creamy texture.

RECOMMENDED BEERS

Coolship Cerise, Allagash Brewing Company
Avarice & Greed, Roadhouse Brewing Co.
Judgment Day, The Lost Abbey

ROASTED BEETS WITH FARRO, STONE FRUIT, AND SPICY GREENS

Cooking beets will inevitably stain something in your kitchen, or on your person, so you might as well embrace their unforgiving beetiness. Their pronounced and inimitable earthiness is a natural fit for Sour, Tart, & Funky beers. In order to add complexity to what can be a dominating one-note taproot, I add some citrus and stone fruits for tang, while nutty grains and spicy greens break up the base with a hit of pepper. All of these flavors will complement the beer, too. This dish can be served on its own as a main course salad or as a side for whole grilled fish or juicy meats.

Makes 4 entrée-size servings or 6 appetizer servings

Bring two quarts of water to a boil in a large pot and add 1 teaspoon salt. Add the farro and cook until tender, 12 to 15 minutes. Drain the farro and rinse with cold water until chilled. Transfer to a bowl and set aside

Preheat the oven to 375°F. Cut two sheets of foil large enough to wrap the beets into two packets.

In a bowl, combine the beets, orange slices, thyme, and ¼ cup of the olive oil. Season with salt and pepper and toss to coat. Divide the beets and oranges between the foil sheets and wrap tightly. Roast until beets are tender, 35 to 40 minutes. Remove the packets from the oven and carefully open the foil. Let the beets cool to room temperature.

Use paper towels to rub the skins off the beets. Cut the beets into large wedges or pieces and transfer into a bowl. (If using a mixture of beets, keep them in separate bowls.)

In a bowl, combine the plums, peaches or nectarines, vinegar, and ¼ cup olive oil. Season lightly with salt and toss. Let the fruit marinate at room temperature for 30 minutes, tossing occasionally.

In a skillet, heat the remaining olive oil over high heat. Add the farro and season with salt and pepper. Lower the heat to medium and cook, stirring frequently, until the farro is toasted. Remove from the heat and set aside.

Kosher salt

1½ cups farro, preferably malted

2 pounds Chioggia or red beets or a mix, scrubbed

1 medium orange, sliced

3 thyme sprigs, chopped

½ cup plus 2 tablespoons olive oil

Freshly ground black pepper

3 plums, halved, pitted, and cut into small wedges

2 peaches or nectarines, halved, pitted, and cut into ¼-inch pieces

2 tablespoons sherry vinegar

1 head endive, leaves separated

1 bunch watercress, stems trimmed

1 cup baby arugula

PAIRING STRATEGY

These beers add a bright spritz of citrus to this dish, keeping it from being too vegetal. The beers also tend to be lower in alcohol, too, which makes them nice for a lighter meal.

RECOMMENDED BEERS

The Thief, Societe Brewing Company
Brett Saison, Beachwood BBQ & Brewery
Bretta Rose, Firestone Walker Brewing Company

In a bowl, combine the endive, watercress, and arugula. Spoon some of the stone fruit liquid over the greens and toss to coat.

Divide the farro among four plates and top with the greens. Arrange the beets around the farro, spoon the stone fruit over the plate, and serve.

MARINATED MELONS WITH PROSCIUTTO AND GOAT CHEESE

Salty prosciutto teamed up with sweet summer melon is a classic Italian antipasto. Don't overthink this dish. Pick up a variety of in-season melons at the market and quickly marinate them in a little salt and vinegar to accentuate their crisp, cool edge. Contrast this with the fattiness of prosciutto and the tang of some soft fresh goat cheese and you'll barely need dinner.

Serves 6 as an appetizer

Place the melons in a medium mixing bowl and toss with 1 teaspoon salt and the vinegar.

Arrange the melons on a platter. Lay the prosciutto over and around the melons. Crumble the goat cheese on top and serve.

2 to 3 small to medium melons (such as cantaloupe, musk, or honeydew), peeled, halved, seeded, and cut into 1- to 2-inch wedges

Flaky sea salt

2 tablespoons champagne vinegar

12 thin slices prosciutto

8 ounces fresh goat cheese

PAIRING STRATEGY

Vinaigrettes are notoriously tricky with wine because their acidities fight with one another, but that's never an issue with Sour, Tart, & Funky beers, thanks to their carbonation. Your palate will also thank you for a little relief from the textural funk and richness of prosciutto, setting you up for more.

RECOMMENDED BEERS

Pale Sour Ale, Brewery Ommegang
Gose, Westbrook Brewing Co.
El Gose, Avery Brewing Co.

GRILLED RADICCHIO WITH BACON, ALMONDS, AND GORGONZOLA

The chicory family of greens, of which radicchio is a member, really lend themselves to bold flavors. Radicchio is so substantial that the leaves themselves can be grilled, the bitterness of their compact white-veined red leaves mellowing out with the application of a nice char. When I'm grilling a steak, I'll often throw some heads of radicchio on the grill, as well, and then top them with creamy gorgonzola and crumbled up thick-cut bacon to take the salad way outside the healthy zone.

Makes 4 to 6 servings

Prepare a medium-hot charcoal or gas grill.

In a bowl, toss the radicchio wedges with ¼ cup of the olive oil and season with salt and pepper.

In a skillet, cook the bacon over medium heat until crisp, 7 to 9 minutes. Remove from the heat and set aside.

In a bowl, whisk together the white balsamic vinegar, honey, and remaining olive oil.

Shake off any excess oil before putting the radicchio on the grill. Grill the radicchio on both cut sides until soft and tender, 3 to 5 minutes per side. Transfer the radicchio to the bowl with the balsamic dressing and toss gently.

Arrange the radicchio on a platter and top with the bacon, almonds, and gorgonzola. Toss the parsley in the remaining vinaigrette and spoon over the radicchio.

4 heads radicchio, cores trimmed but still intact, cut into quarters

½ cup olive oil

Kosher salt

Freshly ground black pepper

2 slices thick-cut bacon, cut into ½-inch pieces

2 tablespoons white balsamic vinegar

1 tablespoon honey

½ cup toasted and chopped almonds

¼ cup crumbled gorgonzola

½ cup roughly chopped parsley leaves

PAIRING STRATEGY

The sour tartness of these beers and the sweetness of the white balsamic in the vinaigrette are necessary foils for the salty, fatty, and funky components of this salad.

RECOMMENDED BEERS

Saison Brett, Boulevard Brewing Company
Apricot Ale, Cascade Brewing
Surette, Crooked Stave Artisan Beer Project

PUMPKIN HUMMUS WITH NAAN BREAD

For an easy (but seasonally appropriate) snack in the fall, try swirling sweet puréed pumpkin into your hummus. If you're feeling ambitious, you can start this recipe from scratch with dried garbanzo beans and fresh roasted pumpkin, but this is a much quicker way to make something that tastes like you labored over it for hours. The key here is to let the pumpkin hummus sit for at least four hours after combining in order to allow the flavors to come together. It's well worth the wait.

Makes 10 servings

In a food processor or blender, combine the tahini, garlic, garbanzo beans, and 2 tablespoons each of the olive oil and water. Season with salt and pepper and pulse until smooth. Add the pumpkin, cayenne, and cumin and process until very smooth. Thin the hummus as desired with the remaining water and olive oil. Transfer to a bowl, cover, and refrigerate for at least 4 hours or overnight.

Spoon the hummus into a bowl and garnish with the pomegranate seeds and pistachios. Drizzle with the pomegranate molasses and olive oil. Serve with warm naan bread.

1 tablespoon tahini

1 garlic clove, thinly sliced

One 15-ounce can garbanzo beans, rinsed and drained

1/4 cup olive oil, plus more for drizzling

1/4 cup water

Kosher salt

Freshly ground black pepper

1 cup canned pumpkin purée

1/4 teaspoon cayenne pepper

1/2 teaspoon ground cumin

1/4 cup pomegranate seeds

1/4 cup toasted pistachios

1 tablespoon pomegranate molasses

3 pieces naan bread, for serving

PAIRING STRATEGY

Drink a lambic or gueze with the flavor of fresh fruit to magnify the sweetness of the pumpkin and the fruitiness of the pomegranate molasses. You'll often find cumin spice notes and lemony fragrance in funky beers, which make them a fine match for this appetizer.

RECOMMENDED BEERS

Vieille, Crooked Stave Artisan Beer Project
Barrelworks Agrestic, Firestone Walker Brewing Company
Bel Air Sour, Brooklyn Brewery

GOAT CHEESE–STUFFED DATES WITH BACON AND SOUR ALE GASTRIQUE

Imagine being wrapped in a warm bacon blanket—sounds cozy, right? Well, in this recipe, a dozen lucky dates get to try on that fate. Stuffed with a tangy goat cheese and slicked with a puckeringly sour gastrique, it's a thing of destiny.

Makes 12 servings

In an ovenproof skillet, cook the bacon over medium heat until cooked through but not crispy, about 3 to 5 minutes. Halfway through the cooking process, add the garlic and thyme to the pan. Remove the bacon from the pan and turn off the heat. Add the dates to the pan and roll them around to coat in bacon fat. Remove the dates from the pan and set aside.

Stuff the dates with the goat cheese. Wrap each date across the middle with the bacon. Secure with a toothpick if needed, but pressing the bacon into itself might provide enough seal. Return the stuffed dates to the pan, seam side down.

Preheat the oven to 350°F.

In a small saucepan, combine the water and sugar. Cook over medium heat without stirring until the sugar turns an amber color, 5 to 7 minutes. Add the sour ale and reduce until the gastrique is thick enough to coat the back of a spoon. Remove from the heat and set aside.

Place the dates in the oven to crisp the bacon and heat through, about 7 minutes.

Transfer the dates to a platter. Brush the dates with the gastrique, reserving some to serve on the side. Garnish with the chives and serve.

6 strips thick-cut bacon, halved crosswise

2 garlic cloves, smashed

2 thyme sprigs

12 whole Medjool dates, pitted

½ cup soft goat cheese

1 tablespoon water

2 tablespoons granulated sugar

1 cup sour ale

8 chives, cut into 2-inch pieces

PAIRING STRATEGY

It may seem overzealous, but Flanders ale is already a bit vinegary and will add to the overall acidity of the gastrique, a sharp contrast to the cheesy bacon-wrapped dates.

RECOMMENDED BEERS

Bel Air Sour, Brooklyn Brewery
Kriek, 4 Hands Brewing Co.
Kosmic Mother Funk Grand Cru, Samuel Adams

SMOKED TROUT AND ROE WITH CIABATTA AND ARUGULA

Living in Colorado, I'm often up in the mountains. This is a great late spring or early summer afternoon snack that travels well for lazy days spent floating in a river or as fuel for an ambitious trail hike. With a chewy ciabatta sandwich full of smoky trout, hard-boiled egg, and a handful of arugula, I can spend the whole day in the wild without worrying about where to get lunch. This is made even better if you've caught the trout yourself.

Serves 6 as an appetizer, 12 as hors d'oeuvres

Rinse the trout and pat dry with a paper towel. Combine 2 tablespoons salt with the sugar and sprinkle evenly over the trout.

Preheat a smoker to 300°F or prepare a medium-hot gas or charcoal grill with wood chips for smoking. Smoke the trout, skin side down, until cooked through, 15 to 20 minutes. Remove the trout and let cool to room temperature.

In small bowl, combine the shallot and vinegar and let sit for 20 minutes.

In a bowl, toss the arugula with the olive oil and lemon juice and zest, and season to taste with salt and pepper. Arrange the arugula on the ciabatta and spoon any remaining dressing over the bread. Flake the trout into large chunks and arrange over the arugula. Sprinkle the chopped egg over the trout. Garnish with the pickled shallot and trout roe scattered over the top. Cut the remaining lemon into wedges and serve on the side.

Plate the open-faced sandwich on a platter and serve.

2 trout fillets with skin (about 4 ounces each), pin bones removed

Kosher salt

1/4 teaspoon granulated sugar

1 medium shallot, thinly sliced

2 tablespoons red wine vinegar

2 cups arugula

2 tablespoons olive oil

Finely grated zest and juice of 2 lemons, plus 1 whole lemon

Freshly ground black pepper

1 ciabatta loaf, split in half

1 hard-boiled egg, white and yolk separated and finely chopped

2 ounces trout roe

PAIRING STRATEGY

The gentle carbonation of these beers pairs up with the smokiness of the fish, and elevates the sweetness of the trout's flesh. Whereas the arugula adds some pepper, the beer adds some acid.

RECOMMENDED BEERS

Gift of the Magi, The Lost Abbey
Saison Brett, Boulevard Brewing Company
Saison, Funkwerks

COUNTRY-STYLE PORK PÂTÉ WITH BEER SOAK

This impressive pâté is quite the showpiece. Break out your most beautiful terrine mold and create a spread of grilled bread, cornichons, Dijon mustard, and pickled onion to show off your work. To tame the meatiness of the rich pork, I add a good amount of thyme and coriander, which nicely perfume the dish. As if three pounds of pork isn't enough, the gilding here is the bits of bacon that stud the entire dish.

Makes 12 servings

In a large nonreactive bowl, combine the cubed pork shoulder along with 12 ounces of beer. Cover and refrigerate for 1 hour. Remove the pork, drain, and pat dry.

In a skillet, heat the canola oil over medium-high heat. Add the onions and cook, stirring frequently, until lightly browned, 3 to 5 minutes. Add the garlic, 2 teaspoons of salt, 1½ teaspoons of pepper, thyme, and coriander and stir well. Remove from the heat.

In a bowl, combine the flour, egg, cream, and the remaining beer and whisk until blended. Set aside.

In a large bowl, combine the ground pork and bacon. Add the flour-egg mixture along with the onions. Using your hands, mix well until smooth and sticky. Add the cubed pork shoulder and mix well. Heat 1 tablespoon of the pâté mixture in a small skillet until cooked through. Taste and adjust the seasoning as needed.

Preheat the oven to 300°F and line a terrine mold or 1-pound loaf pan with plastic wrap, leaving enough overhang to cover the top.

Press the meat into the prepared mold and cover the top with the extra plastic wrap. Press down on the top until the pâté is even. Cover the pan with foil and place in a high-sided roasting pan. Add enough hot water to the roasting pan to reach halfway up the side of the mold. Transfer to the oven and bake until the internal temperature of the meat reads 155°F on an instant-read thermometer, about 75 to 80 minutes.

Remove the pâté from the oven and cut a piece of cardboard to fit over the top of the mold. Wrap the cardboard in plastic

2 pounds boneless pork shoulder, trimmed of fat and cut into ½-inch cubes

18 ounces non-hoppy beer, such as a brown ale, wit, or saison

2 tablespoons canola oil

1 cup finely chopped onion

2 garlic cloves, finely chopped

Kosher salt

Freshly ground black pepper

2 teaspoons finely chopped thyme

¼ teaspoon ground coriander

2 tablespoons all-purpose flour

1 large egg

¼ cup heavy cream

1 pound ground pork

4 slices raw bacon, finely chopped

Crostini, cornichons, and mustard, for serving

PAIRING STRATEGY

Sour, Tart, & Funky beers share many of the qualities of traditional charcuterie condiments, like funky mostardas, tart preserves, and sour pickles.

RECOMMENDED BEERS

Plum in Love, Alesong Brewing & Blending
La Bohème, Perennial Artisan Ales
Sour in the Rye, The Bruery

---

wrap and place on top of the pâté. Weigh down the top with 2 or 3 cans of food and refrigerate overnight.

Remove the pâté from the mold and unwrap. Cut the pâté into ¼- to ½-inch slices and serve with the crostini, pickles, and mustard.

DUCK CASSOULET WITH CHERRY SAUCE

Winter months merit warm duck, and if it's too cold to go outside, you might as well cook something that leaves your kitchen smelling great the whole day. I like to slowly braise duck so that I can render some of its fat to put away for future use. It's also great drizzled on top of the cassoulet when it comes piping hot out of the oven. It's so much better than the Midwestern casseroles I grew up on. A sweet and sour cherry sauce (cherries are a traditional companion to duck) offers a fleeting taste of late summer, in hopes of helping us through the winter doldrums. Thank god there's beer, too.

Makes 4 servings

Rinse the duck legs and pat dry with paper towels. Season with salt and pepper and, using your fingers, work the salt into the legs. Wrap in plastic and refrigerate overnight.

Preheat the oven to 300°F.

Rinse the duck legs and pat dry once more. Transfer the legs to a small baking dish or saucepan so they can fit snugly in one layer. Cover the legs with the duck fat and canola oil and add the bay leaf, peppercorns, cloves, and thyme. Cover the baking dish with foil. Bake for 2½ hours, or until the meat begins to pull away from the leg bone. Remove the legs from oven and let cool in the fat.

Transfer 3 tablespoons of the fat from the duck legs to a large, heavy-bottomed saucepan or Dutch oven, and heat over medium-high heat. Season the duck breasts with salt and pepper and add to the pan, skin side down. Cook until medium rare, about 5 to 8 minutes. Remove the breasts from the pan and set aside. Add the sausages to the pan and brown on all sides, 3 to 5 minutes. Remove from the heat and set aside. Add the onion halves and the large pieces of carrots and celery and cook until the onions are translucent, 3 to 5 minutes. Add the garlic and beans and stir to combine. Cover with 6 cups of the stock and place the duck legs on top. Return the pot to the oven and braise for 2 hours.

Remove the duck legs and the large chunks of vegetables; discard the vegetables. Add the diced onion and diced carrot and 1 cup of stock to the pot, along with the duck legs and sausages. Return the pot to the oven and bake for 45 minutes.

4 duck legs and 2 breasts

Kosher salt

Freshly ground black pepper

¼ cup duck fat

¼ cup canola oil

1 bay leaf

2 teaspoons black peppercorns

2 cloves

3 thyme sprigs

2 sweet Italian pork sausages

2 medium onions, 1 halved and 1 finely diced

3 medium carrots, peeled, 2 cut into thirds and 1 finely diced

1 celery stalk, cut into thirds

6 garlic cloves, thinly sliced

1½ cups dried flageolet or cannellini beans

8 cups vegetable or chicken stock

¼ cup fresh breadcrumbs

2 tablespoons granulated sugar

1 tablespoon water

1 cup pitted sweet cherries

2 tablespoons sherry vinegar

¼ cup chopped parsley

PAIRING STRATEGY

A tart lambic is a no-brainer here, as the dish is already tart with notes of cherry, whereas sours might be too stringent, and funk might be too funky.

RECOMMENDED BEERS

Consecration, Russian River Brewing Company
Sang Noir, Cascade Brewing
La Folie Sour Brown Ale, New Belgium Brewing Company

Remove the pot from the oven and turn the broiler on to low heat.

Thinly slice the duck breasts and arrange over the top of the cassoulet. Sprinkle evenly with breadcrumbs and spoon some duck fat over the top. Broil the cassoulet for 2 to 3 minutes or until the duck breasts are cooked to medium and the breadcrumbs are toasted and golden brown.

In a small saucepan, bring the sugar and water to a boil over medium heat and cook until sugar is light brown.

Add the cherries and cook for 3 to 5 minutes. Add the vinegar and reduce the liquid by half. Add the remaining stock and simmer over medium-low heat until sauce is thick enough to coat the back of a spoon. Remove from the heat and transfer the sauce to a serving bowl.

Serve the cassoulet from the pot with the cherry sauce on the side. Garnish with parsley.

SPICE CAKE

Spice cake can be kind of boring, so for this recipe, which makes two cakes, I dosed up the aromatics, giving it a burst of cinnamon and ginger, and browned the butter to give them more a caramelly flavor. To ensure a moist crumb, I add ¼ cup pecan flour (easily made by grinding pecans in a food processor) to the batter, which gives an unexpected chew.

Makes 2 cakes

Preheat the oven to 350°F and grease two 9-inch round cake pans with butter, then flour them. Shake off any excess flour.

In a stand mixer fitted with the paddle attachment, beat ¾ cup of the butter and both sugars at medium speed until light and fluffy, about 5 minutes. Beat in the eggs, one at a time, until well blended. Add the baking powder, baking soda, cinnamon, ginger, salt, and vanilla and mix well. Add the pecan flour and mix to combine. Scrape down the sides and bottom of the bowl with a rubber spatula. Add the all-purpose flour in two batches, mixing until just incorporated. Scrape the sides and bottom of the bowl again and divide the batter between the cake pans.

Bake the cakes until a cake tester inserted into the center comes out clean, about 35 minutes. Remove the cakes and let cool in the pan for 5 minutes, then turn out onto a wire rack and let cool completely.

In a small saucepan, melt the remaining butter over medium heat. Cook the butter until it begins to brown, 3 to 5 minutes. Continue cooking the butter, stirring constantly, until it is dark brown and smells nutty. Transfer the browned butter to a bowl and let cool to room temperature.

In the bowl of a stand mixer fitted with the paddle attachment, combine the browned butter, water, and vanilla. Turn the machine on to medium speed and add the confectioners' sugar in four additions, mixing well after each one and scraping down the sides and bottom of the bowl with a rubber spatula as needed. If the icing is too thick, mix in a little more water to thin it out.

Pour the icing over each cake, spreading it out into an even layer. Slice the cakes into wedges and serve.

1½ cups (3 sticks) unsalted butter, plus more for greasing the pan

½ cup granulated sugar

1 cup brown sugar

3 large eggs

1 teaspoon baking powder

¾ teaspoon baking soda

1 teaspoon ground cinnamon

1 teaspoon ground ginger

½ teaspoon kosher salt

½ teaspoon pure vanilla extract

¼ cup pecan flour

2¼ cups all-purpose flour

2 tablespoons water

1 teaspoon vanilla paste (or scrapings of 1 vanilla pod)

3½ cups confectioners' sugar

PAIRING STRATEGY

With the addition of the pecan flour, a subtle nutty flavor is added which complements the many notes in Sour, Tart, & Funky beers. These beers also offer a nice break from the saccharine sweet frosting, without holding back the spice. It is a spice cake after all.

RECOMMENDED BEERS

Good JuJu, Left Hand Brewing Company
Sour Brown, Grand Teton Brewing
La Folie, New Belgium Brewing Company

VINNIE & NATALIE CILURZO

RUSSIAN RIVER BREWING COMPANY

When Vinnie and Natalie Cilurzo opened their Russian River brewpub in Santa Rosa, California, in 2004, it was still at the early side of the craft beer boom. Now, Pliny the Elder, their flagship double IPA, is one of the most sought-after beers in America. When they started the brewery, it was called "microbrew," a local-ish approach mainly due to distribution costs; breweries were supported by their resident communities who were happy to drink the beers in the place they were made. But Vinnie and Natalie decided to feed their patrons as well. Yes, Russian River sold to local restaurant accounts, too, like Willie Bird's and John Ash & Company, which couldn't have been more different; John Ash was fine dining, and Willie Bird specialized in all things turkey and had good stiff cocktails. While back at Russian River, they served Temptation, their sour barrel-aged blonde with Humboldt Fog goat cheese from nearby Cypress Grove. The slight tartness in the cheese and sourness of the beer pair perfectly, neither overpowering each other. Every November, Russian River does a beer dinner at The Little River Inn on the Mendocino coast, in conjunction with the annual mushroom festival. Every dish, including dessert, is prepared with local mushrooms, picking up on their inherent earthiness, pairing beautifully with Beatification, their spontaneously fermented sour beer.

ON DRAFT

PLINY THE ELDER

Vinnie takes hops to one of their highest levels, but the balance between malt, carbonization, and alcohol is so spot on, you taste everything in the beer. That takes skill: it's not just throwing a bunch of hops in there, try to brew like that and you'll make an undrinkable beer. It's almost like composing a dish, restraint before pushing the limit. It's so good with intensely spicy food, anything breaded and fried (e.g. Fried Chicken for Vinnie, see page 58), and desserts like vanilla ice cream and carrot cake.

STS PILS

A Czech/Bohemian-style pilsner that breaks the classic European mold by adding a lot of hops. It's almost spicy, certainly floral with Saaz hops, and at 5% ABV, is a great session beer. Try it with arugula, fennel, lemon, and delicate fruit like melons.

CHAPTER 07

BEER PANTRY STAPLES

The following recipes are accents for the rest of this book. A few are necessary components of certain recipes, while others are for those who want to be in full control of their own true "beer pantry." If you want to garnish any of the dishes with hop salt, go for it. If you're so ambitious to make your own beer vinegar, there's a recipe for that, too. Whipping up your own beer mustard for burgers, as a dip for pretzels, or as a marinade for steak—or hell, making homemade beer nuts for Sunday afternoon snacking—will only reinforce the idea of the more beer-minded, the better.

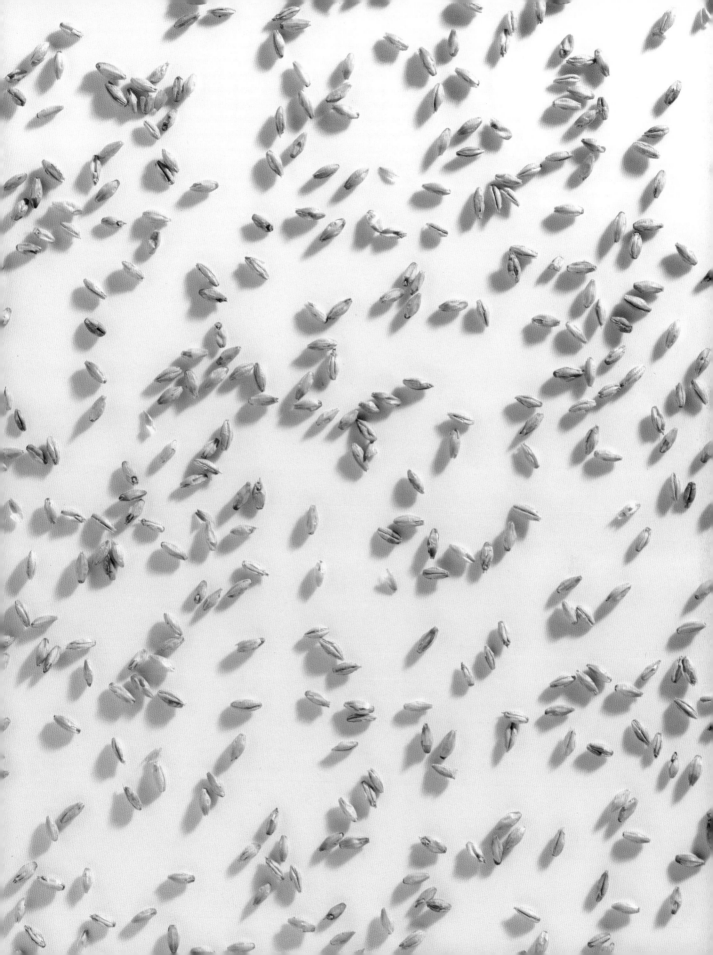

HOP SALT

I originally put together this fragrant salt as a quick dusting for popcorn at a beer event, but there was a ton left over, so it became my seasoning for everything—grilled chicken, seared salmon, even French fries—and I've been making batches ever since. My favorite hop varieties to cook with tend to be Citra and Cascade because they're so aromatic, but feel free to experiment with others. Here, I like to use dried whole cone hops, ground up in a food processor, because the texture is much lighter, but if you have pellets on hand, they will work as well. Hop salt can be used in most dishes in this book and works as a great finishing salt, too.

Makes ½ cup

In a food processor, combine 1 cup salt with the hops. Pulse until the hops are well mixed throughout the salt and the mixture is a light green color.

Transfer to a mixing bowl and another ½ cup salt. Stir until combined. Transfer to airtight jars and store at room temperature until ready to use, up to 2 months.

Kosher salt

2 tablespoons dried whole cone or pellet hops

PRESERVED LEMONS

Preserved lemons are super easy to make and can completely transform a dish, giving a hit of brightness to anything from vinaigrettes, to sauces, to juicy roast chicken, or crispy fish. A little bit goes a long way. Once I've used up the lemons, I like to use the remaining juice to add a kick to Bloody Marys, margaritas, or beer-based radlers.

Makes 1 quart

Slice each lemon from the top to within ½ inch of the bottom, almost cutting them into quarters but leaving them attached at one end.

Add enough kosher salt to cover the bottom of a 1-quart jar (with lid).

Gently pry the lemons open with your hands and cover all cut sides with kosher salt.

Close the lemons back, and place them in the jar with the cut lines running vertically. Pack the lemons into the jar tightly, pressing down as you go. Once the jar is almost full, fill the jar to the top with the lemon juice, making sure to cover the lemons completely. Seal the jar and store at room temperature for 30 days, or until the rinds are tender, then refrigerate until ready to use. The preserves will last in the fridge for up to six months.

Before using a lemon, rinse off the salt and pat dry.

4 to 6 lemons, scrubbed

Kosher salt

Juice of 1 to 2 lemons, to top off the jar

OPTIONAL ADD-INS

1 bay leaf

1 teaspoon black peppercorns

BEER VINEGAR

Sure, you can buy beer (malt) vinegar at the store, but it's easy enough to make your own and the result will be much more flavorful. Hops can inhibit fermentation, so you want to start with a dark, lesser-hopped beer. If you're looking for a hoppy vinegar, just infuse with dried hops after fermenting.

Makes a little less than 1 cup

The process is simple: buy a beer, pour it into in a Mason jar, and cover the top with cheesecloth. Let the jar sit out in warm place—your countertop is ideal—and let it ferment for a couple of months, tasting every so often.

If you don't taste a perceivable change in the first few weeks, add a glug of unpasteurized unfiltered apple cider vinegar to help the process along. Use a pH strip (available on Amazon or in homebrew stores) to measure the acidity level. Once it's in the 2.8 to 3.4 pH range, bottle your vinegar and refrigerate it up to 3 months, or until it loses its acidity. (Left out, the vinegar will continue to ferment.)

1 cup beer (preferably dark)

BEER MUSTARD

I've been making beer-based mustards for years and the range of flavors you can get from the breadth of beer styles today still amazes me. To give my mustard a deep, more rounded flavor, I like to finely grind most of the mustard seeds and then let them cure in a beer/vinegar/sugar mixture for at least a few days before adding water. This recipe is easily scaled up to make a large batch—just multiply the quantities.

Makes 1 quart

In a food processor or blender, pulse the mustard seeds until three-quarters of them are broken up, or at least half have turned into powder. Adjust this depending on how smooth you want your final mustard to be.

Transfer the mustard seeds to a nonreactive glass or plastic container. Combine the mustard seeds with vinegar, beer, 2 tablespoons salt, sugar, and honey and mix well until everything is incorporated. Cover and refrigerate for at least 72 hours.

Transfer the mustard to a large bowl. Begin adding cold water, 1 tablespoon at a time, while slowly mixing with a rubber spatula. Keep adding water until you get the consistency you want. Check the mustard for seasoning, adding a pinch more salt if needed.

Transfer the mustard to smaller containers with lids and keep the mustard in the refrigerator. It will last for a month, if not longer.

³/₄ cup brown mustard seeds

1¼ cups yellow mustard seeds

2 cups distilled white vinegar

¼ cup beer, like a brown ale

Kosher salt

2 tablespoons granulated sugar

2 tablespoons honey

1 cup cold water, or more if needed

PICKLED VEGETABLES

Pickling vegetables is a great way to preserve your favorite farmers' market haul. This way you can use fleeting seasonal ingredients all year round. I use this very basic brine to pickle almost any vegetable, from cucumbers to cauliflower. Feel free to play around with spices to create your own go-to brine flavor. The key to this recipe is to use vinegar with an acetic acid level of at least 5% (which you'll find on the label).

Makes 6 cups

In a medium saucepan, combine all the ingredients but the vegetables and bring to a boil. Turn off the heat and allow the brine to cool to room temperature.

Place the washed and cut vegetables in a nonreactive glass or plastic container, or a pickling jar with a lid.

Pour enough liquid over the vegetables to cover them and reach about 1 inch below the top of the jar. Cover and seal tightly. Refrigerate for at least 24 hours before using, and up to two weeks.

2 cups vinegar (I prefer apple cider vinegar, but white or champagne also work well)

1 cup water

½ cup granulated sugar

2 tablespoons kosher salt

1 tablespoon whole black peppercorns

1 tablespoon mustard seeds

½ teaspoon red pepper flakes

½ bay leaf, broken into pieces

1 pound vegetables, e.g. cucumber, carrot, cauliflower, celery, onion, etc., washed, and cut into 1-inch pieces

BEER BRINE FOR PORK AND POULTRY

Of all the processes at work during brining, salt's ability to denature proteins is the most important. The dissolved salt causes some of the muscles to unwind, revealing more surface area. This lets the brine get trapped within these proteins and swell, as the brine binds to the muscle, creating a more moist and flavorful bite in double-cut pork chops or whole roasted chicken.

Makes 1 quart

In a medium saucepan, combine all the ingredients except the ice cubes and bring to a boil. Reduce the heat and simmer for 5 minutes. Turn off the heat and transfer the brine to a bowl. Add the ice cubes and let cool to room temperature, then refrigerate until ready to use.

To use the brine: Pour the brine over the meat. Refrigerate and follow the guidelines below for brining times. Discard the brine after use.

How long you brine depends on the size of the protein. A whole turkey will take much longer than a few chicken thighs. A pork loin left whole for roasting will take longer than a pork loin cut into chops. Be careful not to overbrine; otherwise, the dish will taste oversalted.

3 cups water

1 cup craft beer (preferably a brown ale, pale ale, dubbel, or wit)

¼ cup kosher salt

¼ cup brown sugar

2 thyme sprigs

3 garlic cloves

1 tablespoon black peppercorns

¼ tablespoon red pepper flakes

1 cup ice cubes

BRINING TIME

Chicken breast	1 to 2 hours
Chicken thighs	4 to 6 hours
Whole chicken	4 to 8 hours
Duck breast or legs	4 to 6 hours
Pheasant breast	4 to 6 hours
Whole quail	2 to 4 hours
Bone-in pork chops	6 to 12 hours
Whole pork loin	8 to 12 hours

STOCKS, BROTHS, AND BRODOS

Beginning a dish with a stock, broth, or brodo will give a more flavorful base than just water (or beer). Stocks are made by boiling vegetables, bones, or a combo of the two, in water, whereas broth is made from bones and meat. A brodo (or what I like to call "farm stock") is made from a combination of meats from different animals. Here are a few of my favorite cooking liquids to keep on hand for everyday dishes. These can all be made ahead and frozen; just thaw before using.

Makes 1 gallon

Preheat the oven to 425°F. Line a rimmed baking sheet with foil. Scatter the chicken bones on the baking sheet and roast for 25 minutes or until golden brown. Remove from the oven and transfer to a large stockpot. Place the onions and carrots on the baking sheet and roast for 10 minutes or until lightly browned. Transfer to the stockpot and add the celery, bay leaf, and black peppercorns. Cover with cold water. Bring to a boil, then lower the heat and simmer for 2 hours. Strain the liquid and discard the solids. Let cool to room temperature, then transfer to storage containers and refrigerate for up to three days or freeze for three months.

FOR ROASTED CHICKEN STOCK

3 pounds chicken bones

2 yellow onion, chopped

6 large carrots, cut into large pieces

2 celery stalks, cut into large pieces

1 bay leaf

2 teaspoons black peppercorns

2 gallons cold water

FOR VEAL STOCK

Replace the chicken bones with 3 pounds veal bones (knuckles are best) tossed with 6 ounces tomato paste.

FOR VEGETABLE STOCK

Omit the chicken bones and increase the vegetables to 1½ pounds carrots, 1½ pounds onions, and ½ pound celery.

FOR A BRODO

Use 3 pounds mixed bones from chicken, quail, and pheasant.

ØL RUGBRØD LOAF

Øl is beer in Danish, rug is rye, and brød is bread. I've had the chance to spend some time with members of the Craft Maltsters Guild, and this recipe really came about from talking with them. This is an exciting time for grains. These days, aside from barley, people are experimenting with malting things like quinoa, corn, and millet, and I really wanted to find a place to incorporate all of these great grains. A traditional Danish rugbrød typically takes two to three days to make, but the addition of a yeasty beer speeds up the process to as little at 24 hours. If you're looking for more sourness and have the time, let the dough ferment for an extra day or two. Eat the bread with cheese, charcuterie, soups, and stews, or just warm it slightly and slather some good butter on top.

Makes 1 small loaf

In a bowl, mix the yeast with the warm water and let rest for 10 minutes or until the yeast starts to froth. In a stand mixer fitted with a dough hook, combine all of the dry ingredients and turn the machine on to its lowest speed to gently combine the ingredients. Add the yeast and water, beer, and buttermilk, and mix on low speed for 5 minutes. Stop the mixer and scrape down the sides and bottom of bowl. Continue mixing at low speed for 5 minutes longer.

Move the dough to a large nonreactive (glass, plastic, or wood) bowl at least three times the size of the dough. Cover the bowl with plastic wrap and let sit at room temperature for 24 to 48 hours. After 24 hours, check to make sure the dough has absorbed most of the liquid.

Preheat the oven to 350°F and grease a 9-by-5-inch loaf pan with cooking spray. Divide the dough into four pieces and press into the loaf pan, pressing down heavily after each addition to condense the dough and press out any air.

Bake for 45 minutes, then rotate the pan and bake for 45 minutes longer or until set. Remove the pan from the oven and turn the loaf onto a wire rack. Let the bread cool to room temperature before slicing and serving.

2 teaspoons active dry yeast

2 cups warm water

2 tablespoons granulated sugar

2¾ cups rye flour

½ cup bread flour

1½ cups cracked rye berries

¼ cup whole rye berries

1 cup whole flaxseeds

½ cup chopped sunflower seeds

½ cup chopped pumpkin seeds

½ cup sliced almonds

2 teaspoons kosher salt

1 cup brown ale

1 cup buttermilk

BEER NUTS

It used to be a given that shortly after you sat down at a bar, a bowl of something salty and sweet would arrive, encouraging you to drink more. This was great for both bar and drinker, and I hope this hospitable concept will one day proliferate again. Until then, make sure you offer some salty treats to your guests as you serve them a few session beers. I usually make two batches of this classic bar snack, one with just peanuts, and another with a mixture of almonds, pecans, and hazelnuts. This recipes multiplies easily, and you can make batches big enough to serve a crowd of people.

Makes 2 cups

Preheat the oven to 250°F and line a rimmed baking sheet with foil.

In a medium bowl, whisk the egg whites, water, and beer until frothy. Add the nuts and toss to coat. Add the sugar and 1 teaspoon salt and stir until evenly coated.

Scatter the nuts on the prepared baking sheet and bake, stirring occasionally, until evenly browned, about 45 minutes. Let cool, then store in an airtight container for up to 2 weeks.

2 egg whites

2 tablespoons water

2 tablespoons beer (a Rich & Roasty beer is good for this)

2 cups mixed nuts

1 cup granulated sugar

Kosher salt

VINNIE AND KEN'S ICE CREAM

As legend has it, one year, Vinnie Cilurzo of Russian River Brewing Company gave Ken Grossman of Sierra Nevada Brewing Co. an ice cream maker for his birthday—a gesture that demonstrates the kind of sharing community of the craft beer world. But it also brought out the brewers' competitive natures, thus starting the Ice Cream-Off—a good-natured contest to make the best batch, by two brewing buddies. Ken and Vinnie went back and forth trading recipes for the ultimate ice cream; Ken uses a little less heavy cream, whereas Vinnie adds some porter to the base (but be careful not to use something too high in ABV, or else the ice cream won't freeze). So, are you a Ken or a Vinnie?

Makes 4 pints

To make Vinnie's version: Combine the milk and half-and-half in a saucepan and warm over medium high heat until an inserted instant-read thermometer reads between 160°F to 180°F. Hold at this temperature for 20 minutes, then strain.

In another saucepan, combine the scalded milk mixture with the heavy cream, eggs, porter, and candy syrup. Warm over medium heat, whisking constantly, until an inserted instant-read thermometer reads between 140°F to 160°F. Hold at this temperature for 20 minutes, whisking frequently, then strain into a bowl. Add the remaining ingredients and whisk to combine. Cover the bowl with plastic wrap, pressing it onto the surface of the custard, and refrigerate overnight.

Freeze the custard in an ice cream maker according to manufacturer's directions.

To make Ken's version: Increase the half-and-half to 12 ounces, and decrease the heavy cream to 20 ounces. Eliminate the beer and candy syrup in the second stage.

8 ounces whole milk

8 ounces half-and-half

24 ounces heavy cream

4 eggs, separated, yolks whisked

6 ounces porter

4 ounces D180 candy syrup (available on Amazon or in homebrew stores)

1½ cups granulated sugar

1 teaspoon pure vanilla extract

2 vanilla beans, split and seeds scraped (or 2 teaspoons vanilla bean paste)

½ teaspoon kosher salt

ACKNOWLEDGMENTS

To Michael Harlan Turkell, without your guidance, confidence, and commitment to this project, this book would never have come to life. I count myself lucky to have the privilege of working with you—especially when it involves drinking a beer together every now and then.

To Nick Fauchald, Mura Dominko, Carlo Mantuano, Olivia Mack Anderson, and the Dovetail team. Your vision and direction made beer and food synonymous—the ultimate goal.

To all the chefs and brewers I have worked with and for, even if you're not mentioned in this book, know that you have my deepest gratitude. I'm so lucky to be part of an industry that learns, grows, and thrives off one another's passions.

To the Brewers Association, thank you for taking the inspired initiative to bring a chef onto your team, further proving beer and food belong together.

— Adam Dulye

ABOUT THE AUTHORS

Adam Dulye was the chef-owner of the beer-forward restaurant The Abbot's Cellar in San Francisco. The restaurant was a James Beard Award semi-finalist, a *San Francisco Chronicle* Top 100 restaurant, and one of the first and most celebrated dining restaurants in America that focused on craft beer. After 10 years of coordinating Paired (née Farm-to-Table Pavilion) at the Great American Beer Festival in Denver, Colorado, Dulye was named Executive Chef to the Brewers Association in 2015. For the past few years, he's exclusively been running culinary programs like SAVOR: An American Craft Beer and Food Experience in Washington, DC, and small and independent beer/brewery dinners around the world (Paris, London, Stockholm, Berlin, Tokyo).

Michael Harlan Turkell's cat once had a beer named after him (Sixpoint Craft Ales Mason's Black Wheat). Only recently, and without moving, Turkell now lives a few blocks away from numerous breweries in Brooklyn. He has also somehow convinced his local dive bar to always have Bell's Two-Hearted Ale on tap, almost exclusively for his intake. And a handful of years ago, dear friends seated Adam Dulye and him next to each other at their wedding, knowing that the two would find lifelong drinking partners in one another. He and Dulye bonded at the bar, over beers, naturally, and after many pints over the years, *The Beer Pantry* was born.

INDEX